THE BEATLES
LIVERPOOL LANDSCAPES

DAVID LEWIS

THE BEATLES
LIVERPOOL LANDSCAPES

Dedication

To Dorothy Lewis, 1930–2010. Diolch yn fawr.

First published in Great Britain in 2010 by The Derby Books Publishing Company Limited, 3 The Parker Centre, Derby, DE21 4SZ.

ISBN 978-1-85983-790-0
Printed and bound by Melita Press, Malta.

Contents

Acknowledgements

I would like to thank the staff at Derby Books for taking an interest in yet another Beatles book, especially Steve Caron and Alex Morton. The staff at Liverpool Records Office were as helpful, friendly and efficient as I had remembered, and I am especially grateful to Roger Hull for his help with archive images.

I could not have done this book without the support of my friends and family, so love and thanks to Jeff Young for companionship on lonely travels; to Ian McCall for reminding me of the spiritual side to every journey; to Reg Lewis for accommodation, curiosity and crosswords; to my wife Justine for putting up with late nights, early mornings and obscure stories, and to my son Jacob for reminding me of the important things in life apart from the Beatles.

Foreword – The City Before Yesterday

'In the early days,' said George, 'the city of Liverpool was really busy. The Mersey was very prominent, with all the ferry boats and the big steamers coming in from America or Ireland. There were many old buildings and monuments, slightly dirty, but basically nice. And amongst all the fine buildings were big bombed-out areas that had never been cleared. Even until the day in 1963 when I left Liverpool, there were still many patches full of rubble from direct hits. Going shopping there would be crowds of people on one or another bomb site, watching a bloke in handcuffs and chains inside a sack, trying to escape…'

I am trying to see the Liverpool that The Beatles saw. A city of cobbled streets and gas lights, horse wagons, winter glooms and summer heats. A drab, crumbling Victorian expanse of car factories and new suburbs facing post-war uncertainties, A Liverpool bomb-damaged and sooty, blackened by hearth-fires and Blitz rages, a steam-train city criss-crossed by tramlines and the clanking overhead railway. This is the place they remembered as children and young men. 'Tramlines ran through cobbled granite streets, and overhead, the tram cables,' said George. 'We went everywhere on the tram, and we'd go on the underground train across to the Wirral. By the time I had a bike, buses had replaced the trams, and they ripped out all the tramlines and asphalted over the cobbles.' This was a city with the strange, greasy feel of old money, of weekly wages measured in farthings and shillings and half-pennies. The coins were smooth and brassy, Victoria's head still discernible. This was a place of men in trilby hats, long mackintoshes and shirts and ties. Women were elegantly dressed in stockings and skirts, their hair piled high.

I am trying to see the band, too, those children and young men, those before-Beatles with doubts, anxieties and dreamy, unreal hopes. I wanted to see The Beatles as children, walking to school, flying a kite with a grandfather or playing in the back room of a vanished terraced house before catching a tram home. I strongly imagined the young boys on these old streets, to the point where I could see them, film-like, in slow motion or as quick glimpses. In his short school trousers, John Lennon ran to the post box on Menlove Avenue. Ritchie walked to school through the snow of Princes Park. George strolled along the shore at Speke. Paul cycled over the hill to an early rehearsal. I came to see this as 'hindsight', this exercise of my imagination, and this reclamation of their stories came to be an intrinsic part of these travels. It was about these ordinary young men in an ordinary city, an attempt to restore the immediacy of presence.

In my mind I watched long-ago city sunrises over old slate rooftops and chimney pots, miles above the empty streets. I could see Paul McCartney at the Pier Head, watching the river, the oily cough of a river boat and the first ferry. The river-basins were full of ships waking up, seven miles crews and dockers unloading cargoes of raw wood, barrels of oil and bales of cotton. I could hear gulls screeching by the river, sailing

William Brown Street, 1947.

William Brown Street, 1947.

high over the white boats and brand-new buses that start, like the drivers, with a throaty cough and a spit. I could see a lonely and confused John Lennon walking home, his hair crumpled from somebody's floor or bed and his bus money long spent on the last round. I watched the old trams move slowly between depots, ready for the day's work. I saw dreaming poets in Falkner Square, asleep in beds still warm with girls long gone. Ritchie Starkey turned in his sleep on Admiral Grove and dreamed of gardens and open space. In a back room on Gambier Terrace there was a smell of white spirit and cigarette smoke that wouldn't go away. Far away in Upton Green, George woke up early, watched the light, thought of breakfast, guitars and that girl on the bus. Time works wonders here, blurring decades, mixing distant years with the present day. 'It was only a few years after rationing. You couldn't get a cup of sugar, never mind a rock 'n' roll record…' said George.

With the release of the film *Nowhere Boy* and some 70th birthdays approaching – Stuart Sutcliffe, Ritchie Starkey, John Lennon – this seemed a good time to pull these buried thoughts together into a book. I had wanted to write about the Beatles in Liverpool, and especially the layer of story beneath the famous places, for some time, probably since living on Newcastle Road in the early 1990s. Perhaps anyone who writes about Liverpool's history has to think about the popular-culture side as well. I had always loved their music and their early musical influences, but I wanted to write about geography and landscape, not about songs. I don't know anything about music and taking the songs apart or cataloguing every gig and every venue was old ground.

From writing my other books about the city's suburbs, churches and urban walks, I was already immersed in images of Liverpool from the 1940s to the 1960s, black-and-white images of the city, especially of the lost areas, the demolished churches and cleared streets. So familiar was I with these old pictures of the city that they began to slip into my dreams, and I would often dream of rubble wastelands, derelict sooty churches and terraces awaiting the wrecker's ball. In a way these too were Beatles landscapes, the city and the band inextricably linked. Writing this book, I seemed to dream constantly of their city: a derelict Princes Avenue, a Mosspits School I have never seen, strange bomb sites near Pilgrim Street. One night I dreamt of a huge Victorian house on Gambier Terrace, a gigantic, imaginary house, dark and decaying, with floors missing and holes in the roof. There were huge, black, marble fireplaces and strange ebony boxes covered in mildew. My brother Martin was silhouetted in the doorway against a spectacular grey view over the graveyard and distant hills. The city of this Beatles dream is the city I wanted to see, the landscape they lived in, their blackened, end-of-the-Victorian-age city, straining forward into the future.

Some Northern Songs

A bus ride out of the city – northwards to docklands, Vauxhall, Scotland Road, the old North End – a clatter to the top deck, and although I couldn't have a smoke I could still dream. In Liverpool the North End means Anfield and Walton, where there is still a pub on every corner, the shops on the main roads are still busy and long streets of the familiar redbrick terraced houses continue to define the landscape. This is how the city imagines itself; this is how Liverpool sees its older history. The Beatles didn't just appear fully formed as rockers and moptops – they had older Liverpool family histories stretching back 100 years or more, older generations of Starkeys, Lennons, McCartneys and Harrisons. Family stories root the Beatles in the city, and their ancestral threads run through Liverpool's broader history. The McCartneys and the Lennons, in particular, have strong links with the north end of the city.

Downstairs, the driver was having a laugh with an old woman as the bus rumbled out of the city centre and into the city's olden days, along streets as familiar as old socks. How many times have I walked through Everton, along the Dock Road, through Vauxhall or Anfield? For work and pleasure I have taken long walks to explore the changing city, to see where the demolition stopped in the 1960s and the concrete began, to see the docks or the streets that weren't cleared, the streets that still work. I have taken many long

Restored houses, Everton Road.

journeys through the older city – past blackened Gothic churches, closed pubs, quiet, terraced streets and noisy roads of busy shops, and roads thick with cars. More laughter comes from downstairs.

I was on the bus to chase vanished northern houses and streets with faint family connections to the Lennons and the McCartneys, thinking to tie these places into the broader history of the city so that their family history, their family landscapes, would tell us something of the history of the city. This was old ground for me, this microscopic exploration, exhumation even, of lost streets, the painstaking recovery of old cobbles and granite kerbstones. Yet I was out on a limb, as some of this is could-have-been history, even might-have-been history. This was a will o' the wisp bus ride into Liverpool's past, into great-grandfather stories, a journey chasing pale Lennon ghosts and more substantial McCartney ghosts, a past the city has in general but not in detail.

So on this warm, empty morning the mystery tour started – or finished – on Saltney Street, a place of walls and rubble and buried cobbles a stone's throw from Clarence Dock, where the boats used to come in from Ireland. The only substantial buildings are the giant dock buildings and warehouses, battened-down sheds behind rolls of razor wire and high mesh fences. This is a Liverpool of warehouses and car showrooms, street markets and vacant lots. It is a street of quiet history, unimportant stories and everyday working lives, and it is possible that John Lennon's

Saltney Street landscape.

Saltney Street, 1906.

Saltney Street, 2010.

SALTNE

Saltney Street, 1920.

great-grandparents lived here in the early 1850s. This was as far back as I was prepared to go.

There are myths swirling around the older Lennon family history. Conflicting stories tell of musicians in the family, American relatives, trips across the Atlantic, multiple deaths in childhood and a distant legacy of Irish Catholicism. With old stories confirmed by repetition, I found it hard to know what to believe. Lennon was the darkest Beatle, the angry one, volatile and unpredictable. There seems an urgent need to root him in a family tradition of music,

Saltney Street, 2010.

especially black American music, R'n'B and ultimately the blues – the Devil's music – as if there is a suggestion that he sold his soul for rock 'n' roll. These stories start with his father, Alf, and his brothers playing and singing in Toxteth pubs, but it then stretches back to his grandfather and great-grandfather in Ireland, a tradition of semi-professional singing and guitar or banjo playing. The timeline runs from playing in pubs to touring America with a minstrels show, to John's career as a Beatle and solo artist and to the musical talents of his children. This is the accepted story, the authorised version, but it has always seemed forced and artificial, even desperate. I preferred the work of Michael Byron, an Irish musician and genealogist, whose work on the Lennons is quieter and more plausible, less wild and exciting, but more believable and more rooted in Liverpool's history.

So it was Michael Byron's fault that I was looking for houses on Saltney Street, where James and Jane Lennon were living in 1851. They were married in 1849 in St Anthony's Church on Scotland Road, where, coincidentally, Paul McCartney's relatives also lived – his great-grandparents, James and Elizabeth McCartney, lived near Scotland Road after their marriage in 1864, possibly the No. 2 Court Great Homer Street where Paul's grandfather, Joseph, was born. The city has a number of these points where Beatles' family stories cross, unknowing, decades apart.

Both young Lennons were Irish and had perhaps come ashore in Liverpool at Clarence Dock. Jane's family, the McConvilles, were already living in the street, so perhaps the young couple moved in with or near to her parents. The 1908 Ordnance Survey map shows a street of very small block houses, little alleys or courts, one of which was Prince's Place, where the Lennons lived. James was a warehouseman and cooper, so he probably worked locally. The other side of the street is still taken up by the long, flat wall of Stanley Dock's warehouses, and any houses were squeezed into the industrial fabric of the area. The Liverpool docks, roaring northwards, created a landscape of giant warehouses,

Spiky silhouette of St Anthony's Church, Scotland Road.

workshops, railways, transit yards and the great basins of river water themselves. The landscape of courts that the Lennons and McConvilles knew is long gone but with an effort of hindsight I could see the dark walls again, the barefoot children running along the greasy cobbles, giant horses hauling wagons of barrels, the air full of smokes and metallic

Dublin Street warehouses.

shrieks. Over the huge dock wall is a forest of masts and rigging, the occasional funnel and blasts of smoke and whistles from steamships and Irish boats. The dock road was closed at Stanley Dock and a commuter roared past me in a BMW heading for Formby, breaking my mood.

The few surviving Saltney Street cobbles look industrial rather than residential, the stones large and solid, the kerbstones destroyed by iron shoes on wooden cartwheels. I wondered if the Stanley Dock warehouse walls were original, if the young Lennons would have seen these very bricks 160 years ago. In Dublin Street, next door, one of the city's giant warehouses has survived intact, a great slab of brick wall pierced with tiny sullen windows and small iron doors. Chains swing idly in the breeze, the ground is spattered with pigeon droppings. Another landscape crosses these stories here. In 1962, as the Beatles were

Warehouse door, Dublin Street.

being smartened up and made more presentable, they were photographed in a number of Liverpool dockland places by one of Peter Kaye's photographers, Les Chadwick. He framed the boys in a landscape of broken walls and burned-out cars, against a backdrop of misty warehouses and rooftops, the so-called 'bomb site' photographs. The high wall of one old warehouse looks very similar to the one on Dublin Street; no doubt these were built to a pattern and hundreds of identical ones lined these dock streets, but I liked the idea that those pictures were taken near Saltney Street, where John Lennon's family might have lived a century earlier.

I crossed Great Howard Street to Denbigh Street and the solid church of St Alban on Athol Street, the old cobbles intact and the rubble pavement a blaze of wild flowers. It was warmer, quieter and more summery. The air smelt of spices and sauces cooking in the kitchens of the huge Chinese restaurant and supermarket. The modern industrial landscape of warehousing and workshops has overwritten the old street pattern here, building over the remains of the tiny blocks of houses off Shadwell Street and the stables and warehouses of Beacon Street. In 1861 the Lennons were living on Paget Street, which ran between Denbigh Street and Boundary Street. The church was only 12 years old, built in the year they were married for the Irish Catholics crammed into these narrow streets. Paget Street has been buried beneath the gigantic modern Beers showroom, a place selling wood and wooden structures. The neighbouring Walmsley Street has survived as a footprint, a ghost on the ground. Tucked under the railway bridge but still defined from Boundary Street, its cobbles and even its 1960s lamp posts have survived. Carefully guarded against theft and vandalism, the land between Walmsley Street has become wild and overgrown. I smelled fox and saw rabbits on the waste ground. But of neighbouring Paget Street, where James and Jane lived with their young family, nothing has survived.

John Lennon was named after his grandfather, known in the Liverpool way as Jack, who was born in 1855, somewhere between

A gloomy day on Salisbury Street.

Saltney Street and Paget Street. The family drifted into the city centre away from the docks, first to Eldon Place, near Summer Seat, and then to Pownall Square. In 1888 Jack married his first wife, Margaret Cowley, in the Roman Catholic Church of Our Lady Immaculate on St Domingo Road. I climbed from Scotland Road to Netherfield Road and Hapton Street, a steep pull up from the road below, the paths lined with hand rails as the old streets once were. The city below me was green with trees and shaggy landscaping, the view pierced, defined, by larger buildings and landmarks, including the far-away tower and slate roof of St Alban's near Paget Street. Away to my left was the black Gothic spire of St Francis Xavier marking a crossroads on Salisbury Street where John Lennon's other grandfather, Pop Stanley, was born, although the street he knew was cleared many years ago and is now a street of the modern urban-suburban houses that the city loves. I remember a walk there some years ago, explaining to bemused residents that I was looking for the remains of the street that John Lennon's grandfather was born on in 1874.

I walked up to St Domingo Road and realised that if this strand of Lennon family story is the right one, then here, like Scotland Road and

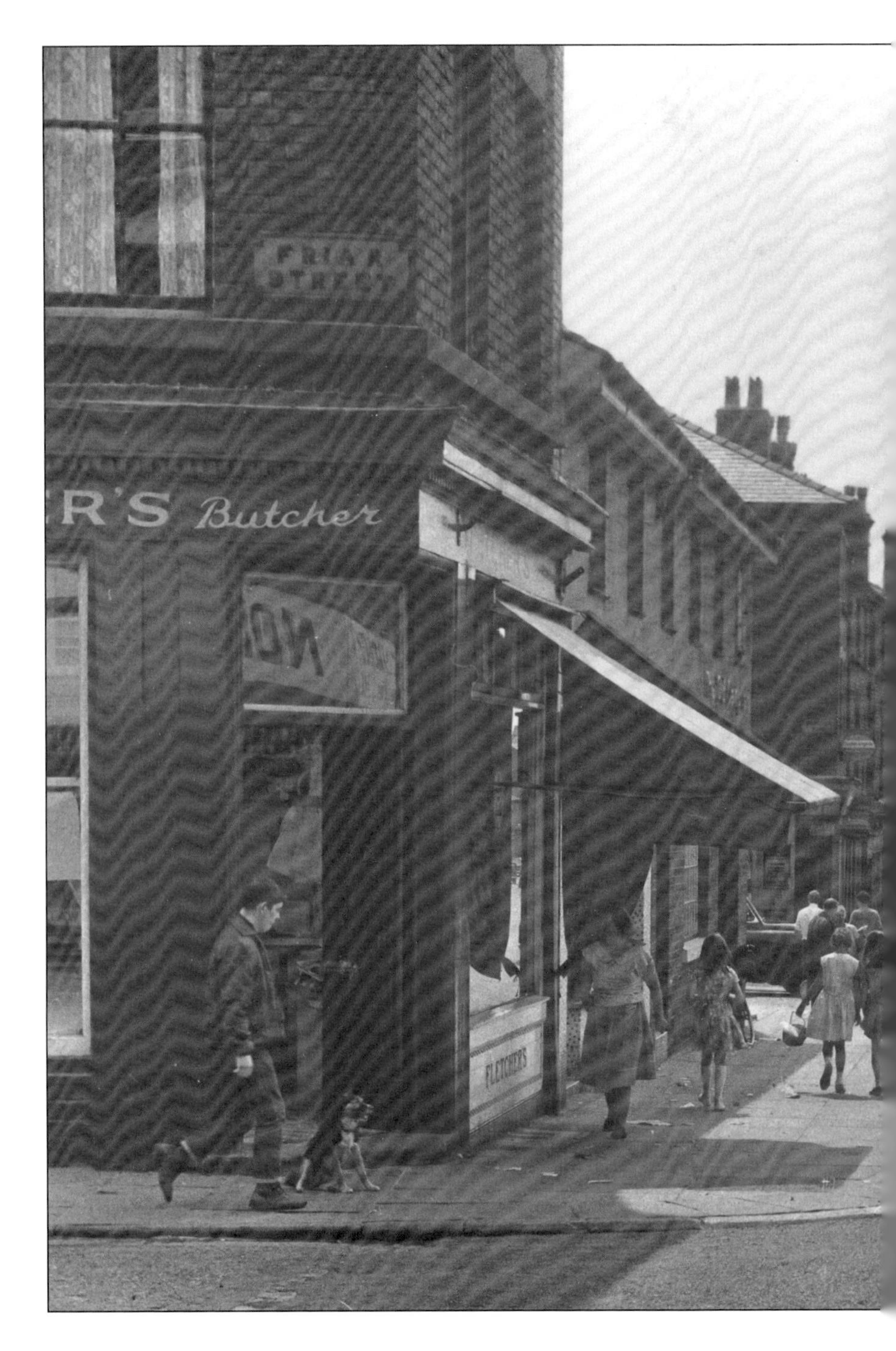
R'S Butcher
FLETCHER'S

Heyworth Street, 1967.

Church Road in Wavertree and probably other places too, is a strange layered history of Beatles' family stories. Very near the site of the old church of Our Lady Immaculate stood Sir Thomas White Gardens, where Paul McCartney's father and mother lived at the end of World War Two, when Paul was only two or three years old. Sometimes these fragile story connections can still be made across time, especially in a city like Liverpool, where the pace of change can happen so quickly.

St Domingo Road becomes Heyworth Street and Everton Road. It seems likely that the Lennons had family connections around Hamilton Road, as Jack's address when he married is given as Stanfield Road. This was an important road that ran in a dead straight line from Heyworth Street to become Rendal Street and eventually join Breckfield Road North. Here, more than the docks, more than Scotland Road, the past lies buried. Huge swathes of these Everton streets were cleared in the 1960s, the other side of the Merseybeat coin, and replaced by unsuccessful estates and now smaller roads of bland modern houses with driveways and gardens. Street patterns were hacked into closes and drives and even courts, and only the old street names were kept to hang on the Close or the Drive, like an old player hauled out to give his blessing to the new team. The important Stanfield Road has become a short, modern, unimportant road called Stanfield Avenue and Elmore Close nearby remembers Elmore Street, which had a later connection with Jack Lennon.

Michael Byron's research has traced the Lennons to Minerva Street in Everton, where Jack and Margaret's daughter Mary was born. I wondered if this was a misprint for Minera Street; if the Lennons had family in this area they might have stayed locally, and Minera Street was only on the other side of Heyworth Street from Stanfield Road. It is now buried behind the high fences of Everton Park. I sat on the grass above the old street and realised that I could not reach this possible, conjectured past. The street itself has gone. There are no cobbles or realigned kerbstones to suggest that there was ever a street there at all, just a modern post box that might have replaced an older one on the corner of Minera Street and perhaps – perhaps – a darker stretch of newer kerbstones on Heyworth Street, a filling-in of a street junction. I tried to picture the curve of Minera Street as it slips down Everton Hill towards Netherfield Road: a street full of women washing and talking, one eye on the children playing on the cobbles; perhaps the occasional delivery wagon or lost van; the step-like, abrupt staggering of the slate roofs and chimney pots, and the view out across the smoky city and the river to the distant sea. The river and the sea are much the same, but my efforts to bring the street back to life faded with the wind in the new trees. This is vague, unreachable history, as buried as the pavements and cellars of Minera Street. But if Michael Byron's family stories are valid, then Mary Lennon, born on Minera Street in 1888, was John's great-aunt.

Margaret Lennon died in childbirth in 1892, so the couple were married less than five years. In 1901 Jack was living with his daughter at No. 3 Lockhart Street in Toxteth Park, near Grafton Street, above the southern docks. He was perhaps a man of some means as he employed a housekeeper, Mary 'Polly' Maguire, but perhaps she was already his common-law wife. Michael Byron suggests that the couple had 15 children, eight of whom survived infancy, an appalling weight of commonplace, everyday sadness and history in that one sentence. As the family grew they lived at a number of houses in Liverpool 8 on Lockhart, Denton, and Copperfield Streets, but in 1915, when Jack Lennon finally married Polly at the registry office on Brougham Terrace, he gave his address as Elmore Road, near Stanfield Road. This was just across Heyworth Street from Minera Street, where his daughter Mary had been born about 25 years before. He obviously had associations here, perhaps good memories, friends, maybe even surviving family, an invisible pattern of aunties and uncles. The Lennon trail on these North End streets cools here, as after their marriage the family returned to Toxteth Park, leaving the other perhaps-Lennons to fade into history. Jack Lennon died in 1921 at No. 57 Copperfield Street and is buried in a common and

Fishguard Close, Everton.

unmarked grave in Anfield Cemetery, along with five unknown adults and three children. Who were they? More everyday sadness, more commonplace loss.

At odd places in the city – Scotland Road, St Domingo Road, perhaps Church Road away in Wavertree – the McCartneys and the Lennons criss and cross like two hands linked, a pattern of families intersecting without knowing each other. Just along Heyworth Street from Stanfield Road, off the top end of Breck Road and close enough to use the same shops, was Fishguard Street, where Paul McCartney's father, Jim, was born in 1902. Fishguard Street is long gone, and here, too, the past is buried beneath neat modern suburbia. I stood on Fishguard Close and thought about an earlier Beatle family connection, when Jim McCartney bought a piano from Brian Epstein's father and the old NEMS (North End Music Stores) shop on Walton Road. I tried to imagine the possibly horse-drawn NEMS wagon or contractor turning into these tiny cobbled streets, the upright piano perhaps being hauled by rope and tackle off the wagon then manhandled into the house before being tuned a day or so later. Jim McCartney ran his own jazz band with his brother, and their father played trumpet for the TA band and his work's band, a stronger musical tradition than has been proved for John Lennon. Whether or not Jim was living here when he bought the piano I don't know. Supposedly, Paul McCartney still has this same piano today.

Jim's father, Joseph, was born in November 1866 and worked all his life as a tobacco-cutter in Cope's tobacco factory. He never drank alcohol, went to bed at 10 o'clock every night and was only ever heard to swear with the surprisingly strong expletive 'Jaysus'. His wife Florence, Paul's grandmother, was born on Breck Road in 1874, a strong woman who was often consulted when families had problems. She was known as 'Granny Mac' around Lloyd and Fishguard Streets. These old roads were finally cleared 40 years ago to become part of the Queens Road estate, which was itself cleared only 20 years ago. I walked from the top end of Breck Road through a maze of small semi-detached houses with gardens and cars, modern suburban houses. They are comfortable and decent, but they lack the character, the grandeur and the sense of scale of the older terraced streets that stood here. Granny Mac's streets were built from an informal grid pattern of larger streets, but the new suburban houses curl in on themselves, creating smaller street-size communities, and they do not seem to reach out to neighbouring streets and the wider city the way the terraced streets did.

The journey of old names and new streets took me along Reservoir Street to Spencer Street and Steers Street School, which Jim McCartney

Cresswell Street, a strange survivor.

attended as a boy. This is a landscape of bland could-be-anywhere brick houses, modern urban suburbia: driveways and washed cars, small front gardens and Sky dishes. There are just a few echoes of the old street patterns, straight stretches of road surviving among the bends and cul-de-sacs, the trees and open space and room for cars. There must be far fewer people living here than when Jim walked these streets to go to school. The old Victorian school buildings have gone, and the school – no longer called Steers Street, as that too has disappeared – is a bright, modern place surrounded by trees and gardens, ideal and safe for small children.

Only on Cresswell Street has anything of these old streets survived. A short row of old terraced houses, no more than six or eight in number, still defines the junction with Reservoir Street. In Liverpool, on these cleared and rebuilt streets, this was like finding the ruins of Pompeii. I wondered how these houses had survived. Once, all these streets looked like this, although on the old street maps the quality and size of house seem to vary considerably in a small area. Larger, decent houses were often cleared along with tiny properties. All too often in Liverpool the baby has been thrown out with the bath water.

One building has survived the waves of regeneration. The gigantic water tower still dominates and defines this part of Everton, looming over the streets as it has done for 150 years, a landmark that would have been very familiar to Jim McCartney and his parents from their homes

Jim McCartney's Everton – the water tower on reservoir Road

in Lloyd Street, Fishguard Street and Solva Street. It seems out of all proportion to the modern streets, towering dizzyingly above the roads and houses, the tank supported by a mesh of brick walls, stone pillars and brick arches. I kept seeing it unexpectedly over the tops of houses, at the ends of streets or suddenly over a fenced-off field.

Odd landscape links dogged me all afternoon. I caught sight of the city centre across Everton Road, and walking along Mill Road I was surprised to make a landscape link only possible in a city like Liverpool. The city radiates out from the river and places on different 'spokes' of the city seem distant, unconnected, oddly unreachable, so I was startled to stare out across a field of old land near Mill Road and see Low Hill and the beginning of Kensington. Kensington was a busy road after the quiet streets and gardens in the shadow of the water tower. It has been a major road for at least 200 years and is now busier than ever. Kensington is the main road and the name for the district, a blighted area known as Kenny and persistently threatened with demolition and regeneration, but the old road itself has a strong Beatles link. At No. 38 Kensington in 1958 the Quarrymen recorded their first record.

This is a famous story, and here I was back on the Beatles trail. There was some curiosity at my camera and notebook from the women at the bus stop and the two lads walking into the city centre, but they must be used to fans here, taking photographs of this ordinary three-storey terraced house, a bit scruffy, a bit shaggy. It has a plaque on the wall, too high off the ground to be easily read, and an etched glass panel over the front door saying 'The Birthplace of the Beatles'. The Quarrymen recorded two songs, which were included on the *Anthology* recordings. Sometimes their music seems impossibly ancient, so quickly does pop music shift and change, and I found it astonishing to be able to listen to this scratchy, awkward music over 50 years later, digitally remastered from that fragile 78rpm disc. This is the essence of lost Beatles history and the purpose of these Liverpool wanderings. Ordinary events in ordinary places are given resonance and magic by our knowledge of

Percy Philips' recording studio, Kensington.

what came next, what these ordinary events led to. There is a strong sense in the histories of the proto-Beatles of Harrison, McCartney and Lennon moving up through the Quarrymen and the old schoolfriends and part-time bandsmen – basically John's old gang, the Outlaws – being slowly or ruthlessly kicked out.

As I was on Kensington I walked to see Minto Street, which ran between Holt Road and Kensington, where Paul's great-grandmother, Jane Baines, his mother's grandmother, was born. Here too the old streets had gone and modern streets of houses with proper plumbing had been built, so I stood on the corner of Holt Road and looked at the building site on Kensington. There are other North End stories, I thought, but they are not landscape stories. The pattern of stories is too diffuse. Like water running out into sand, the stories drift apart the further out from the city centre we travel, wide and disparate, spread and isolated. An imaginary bus took me to Paul's first Quarrymen gig at the Conservative Club in Broadway in 1957 then on to Rory Storm's club, The Morgue, on Oakhill Park, where George first appeared with them a year or so later. It took me along Walton Road, where Jim McCartney bought his NEMS piano, and out along Longmoor Lane to Third Avenue, where Mary McCartney was born. On an imagined winter's night I stood outside Rory's family home, Stormsville, on Broadgreen Road, to see the taxis arrive, cars full of girls and Beatles, Casanovas, Pacemakers and Hurricanes, the 1960s Liverpool bands, socialising after the clubs shut.

Yew Tree Cemetery, Dovecot.

Many times I have walked past Etna Street in Stoneycroft, where George's great-grandfather was born, or Queen Street West Derby, where his son, Henry Harrison, the master bricklayer, was born, a suggestion of distant Harrison links with villages becoming suburbs. My imaginary bus took me to the scattered northern cemeteries – Paul's mother's grave in peaceful Yew Tree Cemetery in Dovecot, Brian Epstein's resting place in the Jewish cemetery on Long Lane, Aintree, or Stuart Sutcliffe's grave in Huyton churchyard. I stood near Minto Close and wondered whether these last two sites are on the Beatles tour routes and whether they should be. But before I caught the bus back into the city centre there was one last Kensington site I wanted to see.

Five minutes back along the road from Minto Close is Kensington Fields, an area of open ground and the Georgian name for this area, behind Christ Church, where Paul's McCartney grandparents Joseph and Florence were married. The church is still standing, a fine, dark, Romanesque landmark in brick with heavy Aztec carving. It was last used as a church in 1975, but after some years as a furniture warehouse

Christ Church, Kensington.

it seems to be being used by a religious group again. Florence Clegg, Paul's grandmother, had to come from Wendell Street off Smithdown Road for the wedding, but it was a shorter walk for Joseph. He was living on Wightman Street, which is now a street of no houses, just the backs of other properties, but it does connect Farnworth Street with – of all places – John Lennon Drive and Paul McCartney Way, probably the strangest overlapped Beatles story I found in the city. From the other side of Molyneux Road, Sutcliffe Street stares at them, forgotten, unblinking. I stood on the truncated remains of Wightman Street and thought that had the city planners named the streets the other way round then Paul McCartney Way would run off Wightman Street where Paul's grandfather was living on his wedding day in 1896.

Relatives and Absolutes

After a cool gloomy day reading the internet stories about George Harrison's Irish family, on a whim I wanted to see his Wavertree for myself. As usual I had left it too late, and by the time I got off the bus on Wavertree High Street I was losing the light. The High Street was a river of traffic roaring between stone houses, flats and shops – an urban landscape, defined by slate and sooty brick, sandstone, cars and occasional muffled grandeur. The pavements were wet, slippery and gleaming, and old awnings protected the newsagents, the corner shop and the butcher's from the thin rain. Was it the same shop George had worked in part time as a butcher's boy when he was young? It was at work that he met Les Stewart, whose band he played in for a time many years later. It was through a Les Stewart gig in West Derby that he met Pete Best. Liverpool links, Liverpool journeys.

The light in the street was grey, sluggish, not much brighter on this gloomy afternoon than when George's French grandfather lit the Liverpool gas lamps. Smeared across the street it made the lights from houses and especially the pubs softer and more golden. The traffic was fierce and unrelenting, full of bright lights and pale, drawn faces. I turned from the cars and lorries onto Sandown Lane, lined with parked cars like beached logs swept out of the main stream behind me. This road was darker, the house lights hidden and the street lamps weaker. I turned and turned again past parked cars and dark houses, walking through the distant roar of traffic. There were pretty houses there, delicate ironwork and Georgian windows, but it was dark and the rain was getting heavier. Lamps were being lit in front rooms, shadows flitted ahead of me down dark alleyways. It was an afternoon for tea and ghost stories. Head down, I walked past the closed Catholic church, the houses flatter to the street now, smaller, less delicate, not so pretty. The street light was a dirty orange-gold and seemed to thicken the darkness

High Street, Wavertree, 1949, the year before the Harrisons left.

Arnold Grove.

between houses and parked cars rather than dispel it. A quick left-right-left turn, confused now in that half-light, and I was on tiny Frederick Grove, facing two smaller streets, Albert Grove and Arnold Grove, where George Harrison's family lived in the 1940s.

John French, the lamp-lighter, George's grandfather, had been born in Ireland in 1870 and came to Liverpool because there was no work on the family farm. He was a farm boy, a policeman, a carriage driver and a lamp-lighter. His wife Louise was Liverpool born-and-bred, and the couple had seven children in Albert Grove, including George's mother, Louise, who in turn also called her only daughter Louise. Naming children after family members is certainly not uncommon: Ritchie Starkey was named after his father, John Lennon after his grandfather and (James) Paul McCartney is the fourth James McCartney in a row. It is the first-born children that are given the family names, as George's oldest brother was called Harold after his father as well as his sister being named after her mother and grandmother. Perhaps names preserve memory, keep the dead alive. Names act as threads, weaving us into family history and so city stories.

The cast iron sign high on the wall, behind a modern mesh of drainpipes and cables, reads 'Arnold Grove Unadopted'. Unadopted means that the council are

Albert Grove.

not responsible for it, basically a private road but in a working-class area so a different word is used. George was born at No. 12 Arnold Grove in February 1943, the youngest Harrison child by some nine years, an autumn windfall. His mother had been a shop assistant, perhaps on Wavertree High Street and his father Harold worked as a ship's steward (like Alf Lennon) on the White Star Line before working on the buses in Liverpool. The story goes that when Harold was home from sea he saw Louise in the shop and on a whim asked to write to her, and she said yes, but I have also heard that their relationship was started by her saying 'send us a postcard!' George was the youngest of the four Harrison children and remembered slipping through the alley to Albert Grove to spend the day with his French grandparents so that his mother could do some work while the older children were in school. 'I had a happy childhood,' he remembered many years later, 'with lots of relatives around – relatives and absolutes. I was always waking up in the night, coming out of the bedroom, looking down the stairs and seeing lots of people having a party. It was probably only my parents and an uncle or two...there was probably a radio on.'

Apart from the 'alleygates' and the inevitable cars, Arnold Grove is much as it was when George and the family lived here. In the cold dusk I looked down the short street – it must be no more than 30 yards long – to the stern end wall dividing this Victorian landscape from the later semi-detached houses and workshops beyond. Arnold Grove is two terraces of flat-fronted houses facing each other across the tarmac. The houses are small but before everyone owned cars this space in front must have made a great safe playground for the Grove's children. I stood at the end of the street taking notes but didn't go any nearer. No. 12 was at the far end of the street, but it was a private house whose occupants want no part of the Beatles industry. Until recently, all the childhood Beatle homes were private, occupied houses, and most still are – Western Avenue, Upton Green, Ardwick Road, Admiral Grove – and I was not comfortable getting too close to them. To me it seemed a strange invasion of their privacy to be too nosy, to pay too much attention to them, to photograph these places because of their connections, as if in themselves they were famous. I thought of Ritchie's boarded up house far away in Madryn Street and the neat gardens of Forthlin Road and Menlove Avenue.

George remembered the '*Coronation Street*' intimacy of Arnold Grove, this supporting, loving net of family and friends and neighbours. It was a regular, small Liverpool terraced house, two up and two down, with a tin bath in the yard brought in for washing. The family kept chickens in the yard as well, for eggs and perhaps meat, with a small patch left for flowers. Typical for Liverpool, even with a house full of children, the front room wasn't used and was kept for best, for funerals and the priest's visits. George remembered lino' on the floor, the three-piece suite, the room cold and unloved. The family spent time in the kitchen behind, the centre of the house, gathered at the table in front of the cast iron cooking range. This memory of family warmth reminded me how cold and dark it was, and I hunched my head into my coat and walked through the alley at the end of Frederick Grove and thought about a pint in the Lamb, or the Coffee House or the Clock – a Wavertree landscape of old pubs – and I remembered that George had uncles who told him that their bald heads came from knocking on pub doors.

Landscape and family meet here in the bald uncles telling Liverpool pub stories to the small George. Wavertree High Street used to be famous in Liverpool for its pubs and especially its 'up one side and down the other' pub crawl. It is swamped by traffic, but these old Wavertree streets are much as they were when George Harrison knew them. Out from Arnold Grove he remembered the cobbled lane to the slaughterhouse, where they used to shoot horses. Above the Lamb I could see the roundabout that connects Church Road with Wavertree High Street, a counterbalance to the roundabout on Smithdown Place, which Paul made famous in *Penny Lane*. Swirled by traffic, the roundabout was as inaccessible as a real island, guarded by dangerous

The Lamb, Wavertree.

and unpredictable tides, and once there it felt unused and isolated, more looked at than walked on. I had the island to myself on that gloomy afternoon. It is grander, darker and heavier than the Smithdown Place roundabout, a traffic island dignified by the Picton Clock, which George remembered half a century later, 40 years after leaving the city. It is a memorial to Sir James Picton's wife, Sarah, the carved stone softened by meditations on the passing of time: 'The slow sweet hours that bring us all things good/ The slow sad hours that bring us all things ill/And all good things from evil/Not at once/Not all to be forgotten.'

I took this public text hidden by the modern world as a touchstone, and wondered about the quieter Wavertree that George would have known, the older landscape and the other landmarks he remembered. I tried to see the modern suburb through his eyes. The Victorian police station on Wavertree High Street is still there, now a restaurant and bar, but the Wavertree Town Hall, where the Beatles played in 1961, is now closed and boarded up. The roads behind the park and the old lake on Mill Lane were lined with older Victorian houses, grander semi-detached villas. The small

Wavertree High Street from Picton Clock.

park would be a safe place to play, climb trees and go fishing. I stood on the corner and imagined an empty Wavertree on a sunny day, pictured the quiet enormity of a summer afternoon, and watched a small George in grey shorts and pullover taking a shrimping net to play in the lost lake under the trees with his older brothers. I could almost see the sunlight bouncing off the water. In the late 1800s the city ended here and, in a way, the old city still does – the old city of narrow streets and terraced houses. George would have known the Lock-up, (hidden behind trees on Liverpool's only surviving piece of common land) and the start of the 1930s car-friendly dual carriageways, suburbia proper.

The Abbey Cinema still dominates the Picton Clock roundabout, as it has done since 1939. George's brothers and sister must have looked forward to the grand opening. He would have known the Coffee House pub on Church Road, perhaps opened by an uncle's bald head, where the Liverpool hunt used to meet.

George Harrison went to the Cubs at St Anthony of Padua's church on Queen's Drive. I wondered why he went there? Was there no nearer Cub pack? It was a long way from Arnold Grove, along Church Road, Penny Lane, Greenbank Drive, North Mossley Hill Road, or perhaps there was a short-cut through the bigger terraces off Allerton Road to Queen's Drive and along to the church. But then, like John's Aunt Mimi and Paul's mother Mary, perhaps Louise and Harold wanted the best for their little boy, getting him

Wavertree Town Hall.

Abbey Cinema, Church Road, Wavertree, 1939.

into an Allerton school and an Allerton cub pack in the hope of not mixing with rough children. In any case, George would have travelled along Church Road many times. This is one of the strange points in the city where Beatles' stories cross, decades apart: Paul wrote about the Smithdown Place traffic island in *Penny Lane.* John's father and auntie were boarders at the Bluecoat School on Church Road. The Stanley family lived on Newcastle Road, which joins Church Road. George's Harrison grandparents were married in Holy Trinity Church, which gave the road its name. And John's original lyrics for *In My Life*, his rejected account of Liverpool places and journeys, mention it by name, as well as the Abbey Cinema. Of the Beatles, only Ritchie Starkey seems to have had no connection with this road.

After the back streets and the High Street, the landscape most familiar to the Harrisons would have been the Wavertree Mystery, an enormous open stretch of parkland and green light in this urban landscape. The

The Church of St Anthony of Padua.

The Bluecoat school, Church Road.

Mystery is a giant field on the gentle slope down from Church Road and especially in winter, when there are no leaves on the trees, it has superb views of the city skyline, the towers of churches and tower blocks from Sefton Park to Fairfield and the city centre. It was the Harrisons' closest park, just a short walk from Arnold Grove. It was a private donation to the city and is informally called the Mystery because for years nobody knew who had given it.

It didn't seem impossible that the Harrisons might have walked across the Mystery to see other family, so on another, brighter, day I walked from Arnold Grove towards the High Street. I found a stretch of old cobbles on the cut-through between Frederick Grove and Wavertree High Street, a survivor of an older Wavertree. This was perhaps the cobbled way to the slaughterhouse, a broken road swamped by layers

Holy Trinity church and the tower of the Bluecoat School.

Newcastle Road from Church Road.

Newcastle Road, 2010.

of tarmac as the old village was by the Victorians and as the Victorian suburb is by modern traffic. But much of Wavertree is quiet and Georgian-suburban with fine old houses, a lively place for a boy like George with a family interest in buildings. The houses change very quickly in a short distance, and Prince Alfred Road across the High Street has some attractive old three-storey Georgian and Art Nouveau Edwardian houses, built to absorb the views of the park and very different – much bigger and more ornate, with gardens and cellars – from the small houses of the Grove. Beyond the refurbished Holy Trinity School, now Wavertree Primary School, the park opens abruptly, the horizon of south Liverpool and buildings a few miles away suddenly appearing. With the sudden vast expanse of green space, this felt like a lost part of London, Blackheath, say, or one of the urban commons.

The Harrisons would have walked along Prince Alfred Road and turned through a small gate into the Mystery. This has since gone as the

George's gates, Wavertree Mystery.

school has expanded across Rose Villas (like Arnold Grove, unadopted) to make car parking space and a place for bicycles. When my mother worked at Holy Trinity School in the late 1970s the old pattern of country lanes could be seen in the grass of the Mystery in a hot summer, a pattern of Pig Lane and Cow Lane revealed in thicker grass or drier spots, depending on the remains underneath, a gentle, temporary resurgence of the Georgian village.

The official gates to the Mystery are stern, ornate and dignified, with a floor apron of hard pale blue tiles. I have always liked these gates, their careful, fragile solemnity, so much smaller now than when I was a child, guarding what is basically a huge empty field. Paths are lined with trees, as if to protect promenaders from the sunshine. It is popular with dog walkers, kite flyers, runners, children with footballs and grandfathers. It wasn't difficult to see the Harrison boys running off some energy here over the years, kicking a ball or flying a kite, or racing to get to the shows that use the space. The Liverpool Show used to be held here, a few days once a year of all that was best about the city. Circuses and fairs still come here for three days over Bank Holidays. The Mystery is big enough to swallow two or three circuses and still have some quiet space.

On the other side of the Mystery is Wellington Road, a busy road connecting Smithdown Road and Picton Road/Wavertree High Street. Here the council have built running stadia, tennis courts, hard five-a-side pitches and the gigantic, angular Liverpool Aquatic Centre, a sports complex and training facilities around a large swimming pool. Again, the Mystery is big enough to accommodate these buildings – and the car parks and new roads they needed. I watched the Harrisons collect kites and bats and balls and leave the park through the old gates, a riot of tall sandstone pillars, lions' feet and stone orbs. Chattering and laughing, the family turn onto Wellington Road. The road is busy, terraced and undistinguished, but George's father, Harold Hargreaves Harrison, was born in his father's house on this street in 1909. Henry Harrison was a master bricklayer who had been born in West Derby and worked later on

Wellington Road.

the new houses on Princes Avenue, according to Harrison family legend. He died too early for George to know him, but George always felt that his interest in buildings came indirectly from Henry Harrison. George may have known his grandmother's family, the Thompsons or Thomsons, as they lived at Wellington Grove around the corner. A large chunk of city landscape has been cleared at this end of Picton Road, and Wellington Grove seems on the cusp of the clearance, a street not quite modern with some old features left. I walked along the dog-leg road onto Picton Road, but none of the old houses on the street have survived. There was no mood of the past on Wellington Road, despite some surviving terraces. It was too noisy, too modern. Turning back, I caught sight of the family walking up the High Street instead of going home through the Mystery. They stop for a moment outside the library and watch George squeeze through the railings to slide down the meteorite, a child's pleasure he remembered 50 years later. They cross the road quickly, turn once, twice, left again, as I did in their footsteps, onto Chestnut Grove and Frederick Grove and home in time for tea.

I watched the small Harrison family group walk back up the High Street, but here I did not follow them. Instead, I walked back through the bright sunshine to Prince Alfred Road and Newcastle Road and thought about John Lennon going for walks with his grandfather, Pop Stanley. Pop left Newcastle Road in 1943 to live with his sister, but the family still had connections here. Pop Stanley liked to take John out, he might have taken him to see the huge tram sheds that ran between Prince Alfred Road and Smithdown Road. These were a major landmark, tall redbrick and sandstone buildings with the slate roofs and terracotta details that define this area. John mourned the redundant tram sheds in *In My Life*. One tram shed on Smithdown Road has survived and is now an antiques shop and some of the gateposts, walls and iron railings on Prince Alfred Road are still standing, but the tram sheds – by then used by buses – were demolished in the 1980s.

It seemed certain to me that one place John and Pop would have walked would be the Mystery, raising the beautiful possibility that John Lennon and George Harrison might well have been there on the same warm summer afternoons in the late 1940s, taken to walk and play by

Wellington Road, Wavertree.

parents or grandparents. I stood on Newcastle Road in the sunshine, remembering when I used to live there and the occasional Beatles visitors we would see. John remembered this street too. 'That's the first place I remember,' he said. 'It's a good way to start – redbrick; front room never used, always curtains drawn, picture of a horse and carriage on the wall. There were only three bedrooms upstairs, one on the front of the street, one in the back, and one teeny little room in the middle.' Much of the footscape is the same as it was 50 years ago, with the flagstoned pavements lined with fine Liverpool granite kerbstones. I turned to watch the young John jump out suddenly onto the pavement, his grandfather behind him, locking the door carefully. Pop Stanley had been a seaman and sailmaker in the days of sailing ships and worked with canvas and heavy needle. The story has it that the Stanleys looked down on the Lennons because Alfred wasn't a proper seaman, just a ship's steward, but then they would probably have disapproved of anyone Julia was involved with. I saw him as a stiff and dignified man, a slow man perhaps, never hasty, from his years at sea and in marine insurance, smiling and indulging the excitable John, warning him of the traffic on Church Road, holding his hand.

Pop and John would have walked along redbrick-and-terracotta Prince Alfred Road, which becomes slower and assumes more gravitas as it passes Albert Villas and Victoria Terrace, before Grant Avenue turns off and the trees of the Mystery appear. Terraced streets of hard redbrick, engineering brick, with hard terracotta detail, run down from Prince Alfred Road to Smithdown Road, all 'field' streets – Fallowfield, Edenfield, Glenfield – a quiet suburb-within-a suburb in the Liverpool fashion. As I walked slowly past in their long-ago footsteps, one house was being completely restored and another was being painted. The dust covers spilled out the front door and down the steps like a tongue of paint. The painter came out in his overalls and waved at me.

There is still a small gate in the iron railings around the Mystery here, near where the old children's nursery used to be, and I imagine it was

Wavertree Mystery.

here when Pop and John came. Pop would have let go of John's hand and the boy would have run off into the huge park, perhaps more likely to fly a kite than kick a football, the child's excited voice taken by the breeze. There is a gentle, poetic melancholy in the relationship between grandparent and grandchild, of time at the opposite ends of lives, and I have always found an extra element of this in public parks. I don't know where it comes from; perhaps it is the sense of time passing in months of Sundays, old people fading and new ones replacing them with new dogs and new games. I stared at the trees and the clouds in this enormous space, seeing the old gentleman and the small boy, each at a turning point in his life, Pop with his hard sailing years behind him, John with his Beatles adventures yet to happen. They stand like a meeting of Liverpool stories, the sea and the music, the past and the future, stopped for a moment to fly a kite beneath a high, blue Liverpool sky.

The Empress and the Admiral

On another quiet afternoon I walked up from the city centre to the older back streets and grandeur of Liverpool 8, a long stretch out to Sefton Park. I wanted to start at Head Street, so I walked along Great George Street to the junction with the Parliament Streets – like many Liverpool streets, 'Upper' is only added after a major crossroads – and Park Road. Past more industrial units, landscaping and a surviving Victorian warehouse I could see the river, and around the corner the gentle landscaped curve of Great George Street turned up the hill into Upper Parliament Street. On this corner stood the David Lewis Theatre, an enormous entertainment complex in its own grounds. The Beatles played here in 1961 at a fan club event attended by 100 or so people, including Jim McCartney. Ray O'Brien says that they had no PA

Head Street, 1968.

No. 1 Back Chester Street, 1912.

equipment but that Paul and Pete Best each sang a couple of songs. Even so, I liked to think that John's acoustic guitar playing could be heard on Head Street that night.

John Lennon's mother Julia was born at No. 8 Head Street in 1914. The story goes that John's great-grandmother, Mary Elizabeth Millward, was left a sum of money by a Welsh relative, which, despite hating 'the

Devil's English', she used to buy a number of properties in the area around the Anglican Cathedral. These were looked after by John's grandmother, and so all five Stanley girls were born at different addresses.

Head Street is on the very edge of the inner-city suburbs, and this area has changed enormously since Julia's family lived here. The old pattern of the roads is still here, more or less, but whole streets and warehouses have gone around it, bombed, demolished, cleared in the 1960s, roads amputated and newer buildings erected. Head Street is a bomb site of a street, paint-spattered, vandalised and defensive. The old maps show the back-to-back houses squeezed into a landscape of tiny yards and workshops. An even smaller street, Back Chester Street, ran between Head Street and Dexter Street, although this looked less industrial. The old courts and atrocious housing were cleared many years ago, although the Protestant church visible at the city end still stands and Head Street still runs between Dexter Street and Upper Hill Street, so it is still dominated by the famous Catholic Church of St Patrick on Park Road. Despite the vandalism and threats of burglary, it is still a street of small businesses and workshops, although I could see nothing of the workshops that survived to be photographed half a century ago.

At the unused, cast iron Church of St James I turned onto Upper Parliament Street, another Liverpool road that is a shadow of its former self. It is a long, straight road running from the docks (as simple Parliament Street) to the junction of Lodge Lane and Smithdown Road on the edge of suburbia. Around Catherine Street, in the newly-fashionable 'Georgian

Upper Parliament Street, 2010.

Upper Parliament Street, 2010.

Quarter', many of the houses have been restored and even bomb sites and demolition sites have been rebuilt with tasteful houses. However, most of the old Victorian and even Georgian property that gave the street its shabby post-war character have gone and have been replaced by low modern housing estates. Opposite Sandon Street a small run of the older houses survives, shuttered and defensive, a reminder of how the whole street looked 40 years ago.

Liverpool 8 is where the inner city meets the suburbs, a melting pot area of artists, students and old working-class communities, famous today as the home district of Liverpool's black population. Today the community is more dispersed, but not by much. Upper Parliament Street still feels like a border, a crossover between the city and the suburbs. Many of the old black nightclubs from the 1950s have gone; that world too has faded and closed. Some staggered on, entertaining the students, but gradually the old clubs padlocked their doors, leaving a closed face to Upper Parliament Street. The huge Commonwealth trade has gone, the ships no longer sail to Africa and the crews no longer come here. The streets are no longer full of sailors on a Friday night, and the city is no longer a port in the old sense; Liverpool has turned her back on the sea.

Rosebery Street, Toxteth, 1974.

In the late 1950s the houses of Upper Parliament Street were caught between worlds. The old rich gone, the grand buildings with columned porches or fine Italian balconies were broken into flats, nightclubs, rooming houses or social clubs for African sailors. In 1959 and 1960 the basement of No. 174a Upper Parliament Street, near Kimberley Street, was home to the New Cabaret Artistes' Club, run by Allan Williams and Lord Woodbine. It was a grand name for an illegal strip joint.

The Beatles grew out of a community, a landscape of social connections and people, some famous, some not so famous – family, lovers, friends, colleagues, workers. Allan Williams ran the Jacaranda on Slater Street and met the band through Stuart Sutcliffe; Williams in turn had a business relationship with Lord Woodbine, one of the largely unwritten black musicians who helped and supported the Beatles in their early days. Lord Woodbine had an adventurous life as a musician, promoter and club-owner. He was born in Trinidad in 1928 and sailed to the UK on the *Empire Windrush* in June 1948. He founded the first steel orchestra in England and was famous for his threat of a cutlass (his 'gilipin') to calm scenes of drunken mayhem in his Liverpool nightclubs. His Royal Caribbean Steel Orchestra played all over Liverpool, including informal residencies at the Jacaranda, and were an early link with the clubs in Hamburg before the white rock 'n' rollers went there. John Lennon and Paul McCartney loved calypso and steel band music and saw Lord Woodbine's Orchestra play many times, hoping for a jam session or a lesson on the drums. The Orchestra went down well in Hamburg, and when Allan Williams and the Beatles made the leap there it was Lord Woodbine who drove them. He refused to cash in on his Beatle links and never wrote a book or appeared at a convention, preferring to live quietly until he died in a house fire with his wife in 2001. But in 1960 he was running strip clubs in Liverpool 8.

Desperate for work, the proto-Beatles played at the New Cabaret Artistes' Club for a week in July 1960, earning 10 shillings each for two 25-minute spots a night backing Janice the Stripper. She disrobed to *The*

Rosebery Street, 2010.

Gypsy Fire Dance but George Harrison remembered that they couldn't play this, so they played classics that they did know, *Ramrod* and *Moonglow*. I stood near the site of Kimberley Street on Upper Parliament Street and tried to imagine the dark cellar, the makeshift arrangements, the teenage Beatles fumbling their way through the classics as Janice took her clothes off in front of them, a scattered audience of afternoon drinkers and the dirty mac brigade. The Beatles also performed at the more famous Rialto and at Lord Woodbine's New Colony Club on Berkley Street, where they could chat up the strippers, drink for nothing in the afternoons and split £4 between them for a couple of hours' work. Liverpool rumour has it that they were wary of playing the black clubs, afraid that, playing Little Richard and Chuck Berry covers, the black audiences would think them derivative and fraudulent. But then New Artistes' and New Colony were strip joints and drinking dens, not respected music venues. In any case both these old Beatle places are long gone, swept away in the waves of demolitions that have plagued this area, and of old Berkley Street only the fine Greek church survives. Borderland districts are always in a state of flux and uncertainty.

I walked from Upper Parliament Street to Mulgrave Street and the corner of Rosebery Street through a vanished world, as the terraced streets that stood here have also largely gone. It is this landscape, spread across the whole city, this landscape of people and buildings that has changed most since the 1950s and 1960s. Yet again I was reminded that

Windsor Street, 1963.

Williams & Port
NEWS
TOB
CIGAR

these streets are how the city sees itself, how it sees its history. Family memories of cooking on cast iron ranges, the kitchen the one warm room in the house, while the unused front rooms sat cold and immaculate. Much of this social and architectural landscape has gone from the city. The city, and later the world, chose to see the Beatles as back-street boys, linked forever with the terraces and the changes of the 1960s, history pivoting on a moment. But as their steam train left Liverpool forever, the city turned from cheering them off to demolishing the terraced streets and re-housing people in tower blocks, the grand dreadful experiment of the New Towns. I have always felt that the Beatles' early recordings, those dark sleeves and solemn young men, are a soundtrack to a city being demolished.

The Quarrymen were photographed here, on Rosebery Street, in the summer of 1957, their first-ever proper gig. The 16-year-old John Lennon leans forward to his microphone, the band squeezed onto the lorry. Grainy Quarrymen pictures show a time of quiffs, street parties, checked shirts and giant guitars, before McCartney, before Harrison, before the suits and the French haircuts, the smoothing down. A long time ago, a long time in the life of these vulnerable streets. Even so, from the corner of Mulgrave Street I expected to see a street of ordinary terraced houses, but there is nothing of Rosebery Street now. I had been looking forward to seeing this street as I remembered it from the 1970s, their first gig being perhaps another Liverpool Beatles story, and for some reason expected it to be the same today. But the Victorian terraced houses had fallen too far into decay and had been cleared, and there were very few modern houses on the street. The old Liverpool granite kerbstones were still there and perhaps the original cobbles, hidden under layers of scruffy modern tarmac. The Quarrymen played at a street party for the city's 750th anniversary and Ray O'Brien tells the story of the band being hired by Marjorie Roberts, whose son was a friend of Colin Hanton, the band's drummer. They played a set at the street party on 22 June, coincidentally nine years to the day since Lord

Woodbine arrived in the UK. I stood on Rosebery Street and imagined the old terraces around me, the bunting and the tables of food and drinks out on the cobbles, the houses cleaned and perhaps freshly painted, the laughter, the excited chatter, the crowds milling around. I could see the band on the back of the lorry, the crackle and thump of the music through the basic sound system, then perhaps some heckling, a change of mood, and the flags and the band faded, the modern street reappeared. The Quarrymen were threatened by lads from Hatherley Street after their performance, and had to take refuge in Mrs Roberts's house before being escorted to the bus stop by the local policeman. Perhaps the local boys were outraged at how bad the Quarrymen were, or perhaps they just attracted trouble; either way, when Rosebery Street had a second party to celebrate winning the award for the best decorated city street, the Quarrymen were not asked back.

Nothing of the street survives above ground, but Rosebery Street still turns out onto the grand boulevard of Princes Avenue, of all Liverpool perhaps the nearest we get to Paris. George Harrison took pride in the fact that his grandfather – Henry Harrison, a master bricklayer – worked on some of these houses when they were built at the end of the 19th century. I crossed the Avenue and turned onto Upper Warwick Street, wider than the surrounding streets and busier. This is a street of terraced houses and newer properties. Like much of older working-class Liverpool, some of it has gone and some remains; old folks' homes built into the terraces, the demolition of redundant vandalised pubs, green space where houses used to be. On the corner of Upper Warwick Street and Windsor Street is another lost venue, the Starline Club, once part of the Warwick Picture Dome cinema. The club was run by the manager and promoter George Roberts (any relation to Marjorie Roberts on Rosebery Street?) who remembered John Lennon in the club, taking lessons in Chuck Berry chord techniques from Vince Tow, of Vince and the Volcanoes. The Beatles rehearsed in the Starline and drank in the club after lunchtime performances at the Cavern, as well as performing

The 'Dickens' streets off Windsor Street, 2010.

here in 1961. The club and the old cinema were demolished many years ago, and the site is now landscaped.

Drifting back, I walked along Maud Street through the 'King Arthur' streets to the 'Dickens' streets off Windsor Street. There are small clusters of streets all over Liverpool named after Irish towns, or poets, or lakes, and in this case Charles Dickens and his characters – Pecksniff, Dombey, Dorrit. During the day these streets are quiet and empty, these dead-straight terraces of flat walls and Welsh slate roofs, the hard redbrick often painted white now, the walls cheered by hanging baskets. People still sit on the steps of these old Liverpool houses, babies play on them while old women sit out in the kitchen chairs. There was a woman knitting as I walked past who smiled and said hello. The smarter streets, like Dombey Street, with its bay windows and trees, are set a step back from the street and were perhaps a social step or two higher as well. I was amazed to find a run of these houses that have been completely restored, the old bricks glowing in vivid patterns. But I was looking for Copperfield Street and I had wandered the old Dickens streets for some time, backwards and forwards past high redbrick walls softly darkened by decades of soot, crumbling now, with their alleyways 'alleygated' against trouble or theft.

Copperfield Street was the family home of the Lennons, who lived both at No. 27 and No. 57. John's father, Alfred, was born at No. 27 Copperfield Street in 1912 and lived here with his brothers and parents. John was named after his Lennon grandfather, who died in 1921 at No. 57 Copperfield Street, the matriarchal home for Alf and his siblings. Jack Lennon's widow Polly lived until January 1949, when John would have been eight years old. (John was old enough to remember three grandparents, Pop Stanley, Polly Lennon, and Uncle George's mother, Alice, perhaps a surrogate grandmother. All three seem to have died in 1949.) Polly was said to be psychic and to have a good sense of humour, and varying stories have the young John visiting his grandmother on Copperfield Street. I found it hard to imagine Aunt Mimi bringing him

here to meet the Lennons, but it was easier to see Uncle George sipping tea in the back kitchen after the long tram ride from Menlove Avenue, his famous overcoat hung on the back of the chair, while Grandma Polly made a fuss of Alfred's bright, sassy little boy.

I spent some time on these sunny empty Dickens streets until I realised that Copperfield Street had gone, cleared in the 1980s and replaced by a tangle of modern houses near the junction with North Hill Street. On the 1908 Ordnance Survey map, the houses on Copperfield Street appeared to have been considerably smaller than the other streets that have survived locally. Perhaps the city council couldn't live with the irony of tiny, cramped Victorian houses on streets named after Dickens characters. As in other parts of the city, the new streets have retained the group names of the old streets but the road names have modernised, so Copperfield and Micawber Streets have become Micawber Close and Copperfield Close. Wandering along Copperfield Close – a pleasant cul-de-sac full of trees and birds, quiet and peaceful – and staring at where the street used to be, I could trace the

Restored houses, Domby Street.

Lennons' homes through space and time, reaching back to lost Denton Street and Lockhart Street, back into Everton 40 years before and even down to Saltney Street on the docks. That one word 'Copperfield' hides decades of lost Beatle family history and so lost urban history, as the old street names do across the city.

I slipped from Copperfield Close to Admiral Street and St Silas' School on the corner of High Park Street. This is where Ringo Starr grew up, his childhood as Ritchie Starkey spent on these streets. There is a strange intimacy in writing about the connections between people and places. The writer is trying to get to know his subject, their family and their geography. Standing at gravesides, looking for old homes, I sometimes feel an awkward sense of intrusion to the process. Ringo is the public Hurricane and Beatle, but it is the private person, the child and unknown young man, that I wanted to follow, so here he will be Ritchie.

High Park Street.

When Ritchie Starkey lived here this crossroads was dominated by the imposing landmark spire of St Silas' Church, which was demolished in the early 1950s. Today the corner is taken up by the playground of St Silas' Primary School. Ritchie went to this school as a boy, although the older buildings were on Pengwern Street, a much smaller street parallel to High Park Street, and it looks as though the school's grounds have expanded since the church was demolished. Ritchie's friends when he was at school were Davey Patterson and Brian Briscoe, and the three lads played on local bomb sites and in old air raid shelters. 'All those bomb sites were paradise,' remembered Ritchie. The lads roamed the Dingle as the Three Musketeers, the Skull Gang, the Black Hand Gang, a childhood world and an extension of family that Ritchie has kept on ever since. When I walked past, the playground on the corner was full of happy shrieking playful children.

One High Park Street landmark that has survived is the Empress pub. The pub is tall and ornate, like a smaller version of one of the great drinking palaces in the city centre. It looks politely disapproving of its surroundings, like a great-aunt at a teenager's party. The pub appeared on the cover of Ringo's first solo album *Sentimental Journey*, his gentle collection of old-time songs and family favourites. 'I chose all the songs I was brought up with,' he said many years later, 'that my mother sang, my step-father sang, my aunties, my uncles, the neighbours – everyone was singing them – you had to have a song in Liverpool.' A strange thought, that the Empress might have been one of the pubs the older Lennons

Ritchie's pub, the Empress, 2010.

Admiral Grove.

drank or sang in, even that the young Ritchie might have heard these songs for the first time sung by one of the Lennons! He remembered a music shop on Park Road, and lusting after a drum which cost £26 – a fortune. All four Beatles were encouraged in their music as young men; although Aunt Mimi was against it for John, Uncle George bought him his first harmonica and his mother Julia taught him banjo chords and songs. 'There used to be lots and lots of parties then,' remembered Ritchie, 'an uncle would play banjo or harmonica, my grandparents played mandolin and banjo; there was always someone playing something.'

The streets have hardly changed since those parties. Alongside the pub is Admiral Grove, where the young Ritchie moved with his mother when he was three, in 1943, when his parents split up. He remembered being on the back of the van with the boxes, and the journey being so short they didn't bother closing the back up properly. 'My Dad left when I was three,' he said recently. 'My grandparents brought me up with my mother, and the house was f***in' freezin', and damp. I had tuberculosis, and there were a lot of duvets on the bed, as Billy Connolly would say – overcoats, to keep warm. (He calls down an imaginary staircase) "Our Bob's got his foot stuck in the arm of the duvet!"'

Admiral Grove is a terrace of very small houses, threatened with demolition and clearance and then reprieved, then threatened again. Perhaps Copperfield Street looked like this. The Grove had apparently been condemned as far back as the early 1930s as derelict, but Ritchie and his mother moved here in about 1943 and stayed for 20 years. I could see that the city had no use for these tiny houses and wanted to replace them with modern suburbs-in-the-city houses, with driveways and gardens. But many of the houses with gardens that had been built around Admiral Grove were scruffy and unloved, whereas the terraced houses seemed immaculate to a fault. There was no tradition of car ownership and gardening there. On the day I walked past, Admiral Grove was sunny and quiet, with one or two older people sitting outside their doors smiling and chatting to passers by, the friendly social tradition of Liverpool.

But Ritchie also remembered the teddy-boy gang culture that soured these old streets 50 years ago, the

Madryn Street, 2010.

turf wars and the violence. Razor blades in lapels, knives, bike chains, coshes. Or 'hatchets, belts, bicycle chains and real weapons,' as John said. 'I didn't knife or kill anyone,' said Ritchie, 'but I got beaten up a few times…I have seen people lose their eyes; I have seen people stabbed; I have seen people beaten up with hammers.' Paul too remembered gang violence: 'The guys from Garston would sometimes get on a late-night bus and come to Speke,' he remembered, 'and they would come, 40 guys from Garston would come and our bigger guys didn't run. They would go and meet them. It was very, very real. It was serious fighting.' The gang fights spilled over into the music halls and venues, and many early Beatles gigs ended in enormous bloody fights, a dark landscape of anger and fear erupting into senseless violence.

Across High Park Street were the Welsh roads, Gwydir, Kinmel, Madryn, Powis, Rhiwlas, Voelas and Wynnstay, a series of identical, parallel terraced streets of small houses. These too were very small houses by modern standards, originally just two rooms up and two rooms down with a small yard at the back. Ritchie's first home was here,

Princes Avenue, May, 1945.

LIVERPOOL CORPORATION
CITY ENGINEER &
SURVEYOR.

Princes Road, July 1935.

at No. 9 Madryn Street, where he was born in July 1940. This was a long way from the preserved National Trust houses on Menlove Avenue or Forthlin Road, even from George's old home on Arnold Grove. All the houses were boarded up with thick steel panels, all presented blank steel faces to the street. Ritchie lived on Madryn Street until he was three but was partly raised by his father's parents, the Starkeys, who also lived here, so he spent large amounts of childhood time on Madryn Street. He remembered his grandmother, Annie Starkey, as a big woman, the 'voodoo queen of Liverpool' with her two potions for all illnesses, and her little husband, Johnny Starkey, who liked to bet on the horses. He was a boilermaker on the docks and once made Ritchie a working steam engine. As an only child Ritchie was the centre of attention and adored by his mother and grandparents, and he was very upset by Johnny's death when Ritchie was about 20 years old. Ritchie's other grandparents, the Gleaves, he remembered as being very poor indeed, with his grandmother having 14 children. The Madryn Street houses were very small, with no back garden, but they had three bedrooms. On my visit even the grander houses of Kelvin Street had been closed and boarded. (The bigger houses on Princes Avenue, on the other hand, were being sold as luxury accommodation again, after decades as flats or overgrown dereliction.)

The film-makers working on *Yellow Submarine* created a landscape to open the film which, consciously or not, draws heavily on these streets and houses. Cartoon Ringo is walking aimlessly through a distorted, surreal but recognisable Liverpool 8 of redundant terraces and semi-derelict Princes-Avenue-grandeur, before he is pursued by the submarine itself, the only two splashes of real colour on the screen. The cartoonists created a haunted, empty Liverpool, a dark monochrome city, a mournful place of chimney pots and columned porches, doors unopened in decades, windows like old souls reflecting the colours of a world passing them by. Forty years later this mood still sat on these back streets. Madryn, Kinmel and Wynnstay were empty of cars, empty of people. They sat waiting to be demolished. On the sunny afternoon I visited, the street was eerily quiet, with no cars, no children playing or people talking on the doorsteps. All I could hear was birdsong.

Ritchie's childhood was dogged by serious ill-health, but he managed some years in primary and secondary schools, where he was good at art and drama and mechanics. He remembered it being 'a hell of a walk' to school, 'a good half an hour'. Well, perhaps, if you dawdle, or have a weak chest. From High Park Street, he remembered two routes to his secondary school in the Dingle proper, where Ullet Road meets Aigburth Road. One route was along Park Road to the Dingle, which seems the long way round, or perhaps through the maze of old streets by Miles Street and The Elms to come out opposite the school. This was probably the quick way. The main run of traffic now follows Admiral Street onto Devonshire Road West and around Princes Park, but where the little row of shops finishes Ritchie would have crossed onto the quieter stretch of Admiral Street behind the grand houses of Belvedere Road. Turning off Admiral Street is to turn into a different landscape. Many of the old streets between here and Park Road were cleared 50 years ago, and the flats that replaced them have themselves been cleared, a pattern repeated across the city and in far grander places. I remember these 1950s city blocks being completely flattened, a few trees left standing, the area an informal dusty football pitch in the autumn and a gentle blaze of wildflowers in the summer.

I followed Ritchie on his walk to school from High Park Street down Admiral Street and crossed Devonshire Road West onto the quieter end of Admiral Street. Many of the streets of smaller houses had been demolished, leaving 1970s green spaces. They were not well maintained but were being enjoyed by some local children as I walked past. Liverpool 8 was a greener place than it was when Ritchie lived here.

New houses had been built on the old street pattern to complement the community renovation of the old boys' club and the new homes on Weller Way, the last of the Dickensian streets running down towards Peel

Ritchie's gates, Princes Park.

Street. Ritchie would have crossed a Liverpool boundary here, one of many, between the terraced back streets and the grander houses on the wider roads around the park. Peel Street is still scruffy, but these streets are less run down than they were 60 years ago when the old houses were awkwardly and cheaply broken into flats. The area probably had more character and charm, but poorer housing. Crossing Peel Street and down the old street called The Elms would have brought Ritchie out at the end of Aigburth Road, next to the tram sheds and across the road from his school.

When they had more time Ritchie and his friends would walk the longer way to school. From High Park Street they would walk down to Princes Avenue and turn right for the short walk to the grand gates of Princes Park. Devonshire Road, Sunnyside, Belvedere Road, even Peel Street – these Princes Park roads are like a lost part of London, the Georgian London of grand white stucco houses on the edge of the great parks. As recently as the 1930s these streets were still smart and exclusive; growing up on the 'King Arthur' streets before World War Two my father remembered the first house on Belvedere Road housing the Guatemalan consulate and the consulate children attending the local school. Twenty years later the area had slipped down in the world and Ritchie would perhaps not have seen these grand Italianate houses, with their balconies and pillars, as being so smart. He loved Princes and

Sefton Park.

Ritchie's secondary school, the Dingle.

Sefton parks and often sagged off school here. Ritchie and the gang would walk through the grand gates at the end of the Avenue into Princes Park, still surrounded by stucco villas and one of the most peaceful of Liverpool's parks, around the lake to Ullet Road or the grander gateway on Belvedere Road. 'I have an affinity with green, the sea, space,' he said later. On one occasion, walking to school with Brian Briscoe, they were the first people in Princes Park after overnight snow, so they skipped school altogether and spent the day leaving footprints in the park. They would leave the park on Belvidere Road and Ullet Road and reach Aigburth Road by the old Congregational church on the corner.

Ritchie's school is still standing and is still an educational building. Other landmark buildings in the Dingle have not been so lucky. The cinema remains opposite the Ancient Chapel of Toxteth, with its wild-green-space churchyard, but the tall Victorian spire of the Congregational church was demolished in the early 1970s and the old tram sheds on Dingle Lane were cleared for new housing 15 years later.

The terraced streets start again beyond the school, larger here and more fashionable today, and a new public open space has been called Ringo Starr Gardens to commemorate Ritchie's Dingle upbringing.

I left Ritchie to his classes and walked along Ullet Road to the great open fields of Sefton Park. Everybody in Liverpool knows Sefton Park – it is the city's biggest and grandest open space, with miles of wide paths, huge open fields, the Palm House and boating on the lake. Here, too, there are Beatles stories, faint and poignant. Princes and Sefton parks almost meet, and it was a largely green walk for Ritchie to go to Sefton Park. In 1956 or 1957, at one of the fairs that still come to the park two or three times a year, he lost his virginity behind a tent, listening to *Ghost Riders in the Sky*!

Stuart Sutcliffe was the same age as Ritchie, and he too might have been at the fair that summer. His last family home in Liverpool was a large flat in No. 37 Aigburth Drive, which runs around the park, an echo of Paris with the trees set into the pavement, the park walls and the traffic. The old Sutcliffe family home is now part of a smart urban hotel, the Blenheim House, one of a number of 'boutique' hotels that Liverpool now has. Paul McCartney was a regular visitor to the Sutcliffe flat, although Pauline Sutcliffe remembers him as being awkward and uncommunicative, especially compared to the cheery and talkative George Harrison. Paul has faint family links to this part of Aigburth; his great-grandfather ran an ironmongers/chandlers on Aigburth Road, and his mother's parents were married in St Charles Borromeo Church in 1905.

The most poignant Beatle story about Sefton Park is the famous story of how Alfred met Julia. Alfred was 15 years old, not long out of the Bluecoat School, and was out with a friend in the park to try and pick up girls. He was dressed in a bowler hat and had a cigarette holder in his hand when he saw a girl he later described as 'this little waif' sitting on a lakeside bench. Julia was 14 years old and said that Alf's hat looked 'silly'. Alf replied that Julia looked lovely and sat down beside her. Julia asked Alf to take off his hat, so Alf promptly took it off and threw it straight

Sefton Park lake.

into the lake. Their later relationship is well known, the absences, the other men, the neglect of John, the failed reconciliations. But this was 1927, and the couple had 10 years of a dreamy, unserious Liverpool courtship ahead of them, with long walks through the city making impossible plans, sharing a love of silly jokes, music hall, cinema, music and playfulness – truly a Liverpool empress and admiral. It is an implausibly romantic Liverpool love story with a soured and familiar unhappy ending. I stood by the lake and watched an old bowler hat fill with water and thought about the strange beginnings of things.

The Wild South

I seemed to have been travelling on these buses for a long time, remembering long childhood journeys out from the city centre to see friends in Garston and Speke, scuffed upper decks and the smell of old trapped cigarette smoke. I recalled mad, crowded last-bus-home journeys from brassy city-centre pubs, the whole top deck turned into the last round of the pub quiz, and aching, thoughtful No. 82 bus journeys to my brief home on Kintore Road, a slow, sad time when I was becalmed, unable to move forward, caught between worlds. Under sickly orange street lights the quiet streets and bright shops slid past my old No. 82 like a film of the city's history unfolding from the top deck, from dark city centre to bright suburb. Today, like the city herself, the buses

A bus on Speke Boulevard, 1960.

are cleaner, smarter and without smoke. But once again, I wondered if character had been lost and whether the city was in some way richer and poorer at the same time.

Jolted out towards Speke, I thought of the tram stories rising through Beatles childhood stories. The abrupt end of the trams in 1957 seemed to me to be one of the fault lines in Beatles history, a turning point from the old to the new, and one of the kicks that made the modern city. Bus-stop stories are also important in the early years of the band: George auditioned informally on the top deck of a bus when John thought he was too young for the Quarrymen; the first Quarrymen tea chest was abandoned unceremoniously at a bus stop, and perhaps there is even the sad story of Julia running to the bus stop when she was killed. George Harrison's dad worked on the buses when he left the sea, driving the No. 500 that crossed the city to Kirby, the longest route at the time. He was also involved in the transport workers' union and worked at the social clubs on Picton Road and Finch Lane, getting the Quarrymen some early gigs. Liverpool charabanc trips to the seaside or Blackpool lights inspired the Magical Mystery Tours, which in turn have given back to the city some of these stories, these echoes, in the form of the old psychedelic buses that take visitors around the Beatles sites today. The most

Speke landscape.

famous bus story is how Paul and George met, the only two boys on the No. 86 or the No. 82 in Liverpool Institute uniforms, or the only two Institute boys carrying musical instruments. This was another hidden 1950s landscape, this absence of private cars.

Leaving Garston, the sky seemed to open up around me. The modern industrial landscape is lower, built further back from the road and screened by trees. The sky is more important here, the sky is bigger, as George Harrison noticed. Heading for Speke, the city's industrial estates and parks seem full of trees, greenery, birdsong and open space. Wherever I went in the city on all of these Beatle meanderings, these Beatlings, everywhere seemed to echo with birdsong. It has many faults and many problems, but the city is cleaner and greener than it was half a century ago.

The bus dropped me on Speke Boulevard, which is lined with trees and is maniacally busy with traffic. It is one of south Liverpool's major artery roads. Speke seems a strange place to hunt for Beatles history. It seems too modern, too contemporary, too much a part of Liverpool's 20th-century history. It looks forward to the modern suburbs of driveways and cars, hanging baskets and satellite dishes. There seems no room here for black-and-white back-street Beatles – this is a district that has already made the leap into suburbia. But the Beatles and their family stories reflect a Liverpool journey from the Irish boats to the back streets, to better back streets and out into sunny suburbia. Only Ringo is firmly rooted in that Victorian landscape of small terraced houses.

I walked from the Boulevard down into Speke along Western Avenue. Paul's family – Jim, Mary, Paul and Michael – left the old city behind them forever in 1946 when they moved to Western Avenue. This was the first family home that Paul remembered; he would have been three or four and Michael would have only been two years old. Paul's earliest memory was of watching his mother cycle away through thick snow to attend a birth, but No. 72 Western Avenue was the last 'midwife' house they lived in – Mary resigned during her time here to spend more time

Western Avenue.

with the boys and not be out at night. Western Avenue is a broad avenue lined with trees, a mid-20th-century dual carriageway that anticipated more cars on the roads. Most houses in Speke have at least one car in the driveway these days, but the roads still seem wide, pleasantly empty, easy to drive. Officially, Speke is a 'township' intended as a self-contained community, and it won awards in the 1930s for the city planners. George remembered that in the early years the buses didn't go into the township, so they got off on the Boulevard and walked for 10 or 20 minutes to home. The landscape feels open and generous, a place of wide streets and space between houses, gardens and trees, grassland becoming fields.

'We always felt like a pioneer family in a wagon train,' said Paul. 'They were frontiers, the outskirts of Liverpool, where we were sent.' Speke was the wild south. When the McCartneys moved there the township was still in the process of construction, and Paul remembers the roads were still being built. Building on Speke stopped during World War Two and began again in the 1950s, so the township in the late 1940s must have felt half-finished. Paul went to Stockton Wood School, behind Western

Upton Green.

Avenue, but as the population grew the school was swamped with new pupils, and Paul was one of the children who were taken by bus to Joseph Williams Primary School in Belle Vale, another growing district. This was a time of rapid development for these huge new suburbs. Everything must have felt new, moving forward in fits and starts. The churches, too, were incomplete, and as one of a Catholic family George Harrison remembered the priest coming to the house fundraising for the new churches, which would be St Christopher's or the grander and more impressive St Ambrose's.

George's family had finally reached the top of the Corporation's housing list in 1950, when Harold and Louise, and their children moved from Arnold Grove to a modern house in Speke, although George stayed at Dovedale Road School. Upton Green is a quieter and more secluded address than Western Avenue, tucked away off Little Heath Road, one of the 'new council houses out there with bathrooms and kitchens,' as George said. Upton Green must have felt a world away from Arnold Grove – bright, modern, with a garden front and back. Beatles legend has it that

George loved the huge skies and wide open spaces of Speke but that his mother missed the intimacy and friendliness of Arnold Grove, having spent all her life there or on the neighbouring Albert Grove. Louise was one of the Beatle parents who encouraged their music, and the Quarrymen often rehearsed at the house in Upton Green. The trees are older and more settled and as usual there are more cars on the roads and more white plastic windows and doors, but these streets are very similar to how they were 50 years ago. I didn't find it difficult to imagine the young Quarrymen, all blazers and greased-back hair, lumping their makeshift instruments from the bus stop to Upton Green, although by the time they rehearsed here they were moving into guitars and looking for a drummer. 'After a while there was only John, Paul and me left,' said George.

When Mary resigned in April 1950 the McCartneys moved again in Speke, to No. 12 Ardwick Road, not as busy as Western Avenue, and dominated today by a huge open field that takes up almost one side of the street. Were there houses here once or has this great space always been here? When the McCartneys moved in the road was unfinished, and Paul remembers slopping through the muddy street for a year. It is a quiet road, and on my walk the only person I saw on Ardwick Road was the postman.

Speke still feels like the very edge of the city, like a town on a border or a frontier. There is a clear boundary here between urban and rural. I have walked a lot through Speke, researching landscape for a book on the city's suburbs, finding the old farm tracks that had been straightened into suburban roads, tracing the old road names that commemorate vanished farms. The giant hay wagons still rumble through Speke in the late summer, and the township – built on flat fields – is surrounded by open spaces. The new city airport, named, of course, after John Lennon, provides acres of green space, even if it is inaccessible to people. The birds don't know that, though, and the sky was full of skylarks and early swifts when I walked there. Paul and George both loved the contrast between the urban landscape of Speke's roads and the farmland around it. 'I would walk for miles along the mud cliffs of the Mersey and through

The Mersey at Oglet.

farms and fields,' said George, who also remembered ponds filled with sticklebacks and games in the Halewood fields before the giant Ford factory was built. Paul's family went for long walks to the lighthouse at Hale Point, and both Beatles remembered walking down Dungeon Lane to the Mersey shore at Oglet, one of a string of lost fishing villages along these upper reaches of the river. It was easy to be out in real countryside here with a sense of true wild peace, not managed municipal parks.

Tank traps and clouds, Oglet.

George and Paul's Speke homes were very different from homes they had had before. I walked through the township from Upton Green to Dungeon Lane, the very edge of the city. The lane is neglected, pot-holed and badly repaired, but it runs out into real fields, under skies full of birds. The township stops abruptly on Hale Road, and I could see the low roofs and occasional spires of Speke fall back into the landscape of green fields and huge blue skies. The extensions to Speke Airport stop just short of Dungeon Lane, so some of the farm fields are now neatly cut grass and criss-crossed with runways, but beyond the landing lights I walked past fields of vegetables on the road running down to the river. A modern nature reserve or country park seems to have failed here and the neat fences and concrete gateways are broken and overgrown, the pathways churned by bicycles and hammered by winter rains. The road surface is scruffy and badly maintained, like a road in a war zone, perhaps deliberately barely passable. But no amount of human abuse can compete with nature, and the human failures here only make these shore fields all the wilder, all the more natural. It is still exhilarating to follow a small path out of the bushes onto the low heights above the river and see the hills of Frodsham on the distant Cheshire shore, a mile or more away across the sparkling, indifferent water.

There is a darker side to Speke. The township was always too dependent on the giant factories it was built to serve, and employment suffered when they closed. Speke has struggled to shrug off its reputation for crime and antisocial behaviour. It is still a watchful, wary place today, the boys shaven-headed, perfecting their Liverpool frowns. Both young Beatles experienced some 'nasty moments', as George put it. 'I was looking out for guys on every corner who were going to beat me up,' Paul said. He was mugged on one walk down by the river and his watch was stolen, but he knew the boys who had done it and testified against them in court. George remembers a darker mood, an underlying presence on the streets. He remembered the mudflats at low tide being churned up by people on motorcycles, the forerunners of today's quad bikes and trials bikes. He also remembered other families breaking up, families with too many children and other people's illicit sexual affairs. On a number of occasions his mother had to throw a bucket of water over someone who came to the house 'cursing and swearing', but intriguingly he doesn't go into details, which perhaps he either didn't know or didn't remember.

There are few Beatles ghosts in bright, modern, problematic Speke. On a quiet moment I pictured the Quarrymen walking along Little Heath Road and turning into Upton Green, laughing and joking. I found it difficult to imagine Paul and George here and could not see the young George on his bicycle heading for Forthlin Road with his guitar on his back, but down on the shore I could easily see the McCartney family walking towards Hale. I could hear the family jokes, the fun of being together, and saw them looking at clouds, wildflowers and the birds out on the mudflats. I could see George, perhaps with his brothers, older now than the boy who took his shrimp net to the park in Wavertree, tramping along Dungeon Lane after a day on the shore, filthy and tired, heading home for tea in Upton Green. I followed them back up through Speke and onto the Boulevard, knowing I would see no Institute uniforms but still hoping for a lift from Mr Harrison's bus.

Paul McCartney in Allerton

Over the years I have had many friends who have lived in the rather heavy flats around Sefton Park, the solid Victorian villas broken into apartments in the 1960s. I remember nights in the bars and restaurants of Lark Lane, long afternoons drinking in Keith's, or the bright greenery of the Albert pub on the thin studenty edge of Liverpool bohemia. These were days that ended in bags of chips and cheap bottles of wine, warm evenings and the summer windows wide open for the birdsong. After a half-night's half-sleep I have walked home to Allerton and Newcastle Road many times through Sefton Park and along a silent, empty Penny Lane. I wanted to put this famous street into its broader context so for memory's sake I walked this route again from an old friend's house up into Allerton, starting – for old time's sake – at about 5am.

The empty streets were full of a soft grey light, a just-before-July-dawn light, the trees in the park just starting to appear through the fog. It was quiet enough to hear my own footsteps. Everywhere was still, haunted by early birdsong and the city's distant hum. I stood by the lake and remembered coming here with my father and grandfather, sailing paper boats and wooden yachts. A thin mist rose from the water. As I walked through the old park alone I thought of Beatle-teenagers having sex and throwing bowler hats into the lake, and of Stuart Sutcliffe asleep on Aigburth Park Drive. As the light strengthened I turned past Greenbank Park and again at the halls of residence. It was too early for runners and dog walkers. I pictured the students in their sleep as I turned again onto the rural end of Penny Lane. I must have walked down this road 100 times.

It was too early for the tourists, the Beatles pilgrims, and the Magical Mystery Tour buses. There were just trees full of uncertain, hesitant birds starting to sing cautiously, as if unsure of the light. I stood in the middle of the Lane and stared at the absence of cars. The famous black and white road sign has been painted onto the sandstone wall here after the old ones (and all their replacements) were stolen over the years. The original iron ones, which were here in the 1960s, the ones Paul McCartney saw, must now be worth their weight in gold.

At this end of Penny Lane the thick trees of Sefton and Greenbank parks have jumped the railings and spilled into the surrounding streets, the old 'country' estates and large gardens creating a landscape of trees and greenery with the familiar south Liverpool ingredients of beech trees and sandstone walls. Early in the morning, with a slight dawn mist and no sound but the birds, these old roads seem to be remembering the country lanes they used to be. This end of Penny Lane seems more rural because of the ruffle of tall trees and the open playing fields beyond the low sandstone wall, and the large houses sleeping behind yet more trees. For an urban landscape, these streets are defined by mature trees. Beeches, chestnuts and oaks rise as the land lifts towards Mossley Hill, creating a view of forest trees and church towers. Over the empty playing fields and distant trees of Queen's Drive I could see the Italian church tower of St Anthony of Padua, where George Harrison was in the Cubs. It is a long way from Arnold Grove.

A pattern of small streets appeared on my left, one of many hidden tumbles of

Penny Lane landscape – the wine bar and St Barnabas church.

Penny Lane, April 1936.

Penny Lane.

streets in the city where smaller and smaller streets seem to open up like Chinese boxes from one larger street. A taxi appeared, breaking the silence, switching his 'for hire' light off when he saw me and hastily turning down Penny Lane. Not that I wanted a cab. The Lane starts to pull up here as it takes the bridge over the railway line, and the playing fields end abruptly. The landscape from the top of the railway bridge was pure south Liverpool, perhaps typical of the city's older suburbs – a calm redbrick sea of slate roofs and redundant chimney stacks, stands of trees, the occasional sandstone spire of a distant church. The bridge looked fairly modern, but this railway line was the Intercity route to London, and on the boys' first visit to the capital as Beatles, with Brian Epstein in late 1961, their steam train would have passed under this bridge, adding another layer of soot. I could see all of Penny Lane from up there. The railway marked the fine line between the rural south Liverpool of parks and large gardens, and the urban south Liverpool of redbrick terraced streets. To my left, the logical, even pattern of terraces unfolded – jagged but almost uninterrupted – into the city centre a couple of miles away, and to my right there was a further great swathe of the terraces along Allerton Road and down towards Rose Lane and Aigburth Road.

The light was stronger now, the birdsong louder and more confident. A milkman waved as he passed me in his float, that curious mixture of humming electric engine and rattling glass bottles. Walking on, I could see the end of Penny Lane, the austere Welsh church on Smithdown Place, empty now and sprouting weeds like an old man's whiskers. On the left of the lane were fine terraced streets of hard Liverpool redbrick, but to the right were the trees, bigger houses and the school of Dovedale Road. John Lennon and George Harrison were pupils here, before they knew each other. On the corner, with its curious Italian tower and stopped clock, was Dovedale Towers, an old country house marooned in suburbia. It has a long history and has been a pub, restaurant, social club, and a home for incurable children. In 1957, when the Quarrymen played here, it was the parish hall for St Barnabas's Church.

Smithdown Place, October 1956.

One side of the street had fine large terraced houses, the other had a high sandstone wall hiding a scruffy expanse of grass. A fine curve of entrance suggested that another old house once stood here, a house that had not survived. I remembered THE BEATLES and THE WHO painted onto these elegant stones in very faded letters, perhaps graffiti as old as the 1960s. Nearer the main road now and another little flurry of hidden streets appeared on my right, along with two shops, the old Penny Lane Records store – another lost Liverpool institution – and the lively Penny Lane Wine Bar. It wasn't lively at this time, though, closed and shuttered, the last drinker gone home hours before. St Barnabas Church tower loomed up on my right, solid and disapproving of my late or early meanderings, like an old-fashioned policeman. Michael McCartney was married here in the early 1980s, close enough to the 1950s for the vicar to remember Paul singing in the choir.

Penny Lane ends at a complicated junction where Allerton Road, Smithdown Road, Heathfield Road and Church Road all meet. The

Victorians elegantly simplified this knot into Smithdown Place, around the shelter in the middle of the roundabout. 'Penny Lane' now means this whole area, nobody calls it Smithdown Place any more. I crossed Allerton Road just behind the newspaper delivery lorry. I slipped a newspaper awkwardly from the stringed bundle outside the shop and left the money on top of the pile.

The Smithdown Place end of Penny Lane is built-up and urban, very different in mood from the other end under the trees near the parks. It was still very early and the shelter in the middle of the roundabout was quiet and empty. The buses that rolled across the city wouldn't start for another hour or so, and until then Smithdown Place would be shabby and deserted, a landscape of overworked and weary Victoriana of tall redbrick buildings, a roofline of urns and balconies, carvings and ornate doorways. Taxis passed occasionally, either slowing for business or hurrying home at the end of a long night. This is also a landscape defined by the elements in the song, of course, although the chip shop and the bank were closed, and the barber shop wouldn't open until 8.30.

The shelter in the middle of the roundabout, Smithdown Place, 2010.

The fire station was at the other end of Allerton Road, and the pretty nurse was asleep somewhere, worrying about her grandchildren. The birds had a chance to sing.

These are fascinatingly ordinary places. Penny Lane and the roundabout is not a rock shrine like Strawberry Field, graffitied and respected, it is an undistinguished road junction and bus terminus. Most of the day it is choked with cars, traffic coming from Church Road and Smithdown Road, joining Allerton Road, following the taxi cabs down Penny Lane to avoid the jams. The attractive buildings are dwarfed by ugly street lighting and traffic bollards. I wondered what the Beatles pilgrims make of it all, swinging round the bus stops in the Magical Mystery Tour bus. Perhaps its very English ordinariness, even the fact that there is nothing here, is what is attractive about it – 'Yeah, I saw Penny Lane, Mom, and guess what? There's nothing there!' Even on a quiet morning, the past too was difficult to conjure. I tried to picture Paul here, changing buses or walking up to the cinema, or John's pale, owl face staring out of the bus window as the No. 5 rumbles through towards town. I tried to see George trudging slowly to his Cubs meeting on a rainy day with no lift or bus money, down Church Road and fading on to Penny Lane, but the roundabout was too familiar, too much a part of my life as much as theirs.

Sitting on the roundabout in the faint patterings of early traffic, I remembered John's response to *Penny Lane.* An early draft of *In My Life* has survived and once I found it, unexpectedly, on show at the British Museum, a little piece of Liverpool street life, out of

The other bank, Smithdown Place, 2010.

Smithdown Road tramcar sheds, remembered by John Lennon in the original draft of *In My Life*.

context and full of incomprehensible references, in a glass case in London. Was it a response? Which came first, I wondered? Lennon later scornfully dismissed this as a travelogue and rewrote the song completely, but it was interesting to me as a topographical song, a lost account of Liverpool journeys. 'Penny Lane is one I'm missing/up Church Road to the clock tower/in the circle of the Abbey/I have seen some happy hours,' he wrote, describing the landscape that George Harrison grew up in. A second verse remembers the journey along Smithdown Road into town: 'Past the tram sheds with no trams/on the 5 bus into town/Past the Dutchy and St Columba's/to the Dockers' Umbrella that they pulled down.' John would have remembered the tram sheds on Prince Alfred Road from his visits to Newcastle Road and the last Liverpool tram running when he was 17. He would have caught the No. 5 bus into Liverpool city centre from Menlove Avenue, and – a macabre thought – it could have been a No. 5 that Julia was going to catch when she was run over and killed. St Columba's Church tower

John Lennon's Smithdown Road, 1959.

survives on Smithdown Road, although the Dutchy café, with its small wooden windmill above the door, has gone. 'The Dockers' Umbrella' was a facetious nickname for the Overhead Railway that ran along the Liverpool docks until it was torn down in the late 1950s. The No. 5 bus ran in those days to the Pier Head and the river, the very edge of the city.

The day was waking up. The sun broke through the clouds, and a shop shutter rattled somewhere behind me. An old man walked across Church Road with an excited small boy. As I sat and thought, an old No. 86 bus appeared, rumbling slowly out of Smithdown Road towards me. The bus stopped, and the driver took my money without a word. I climbed the stairs and took the periscope seat at the front, the one with the view of the driver's head. The upper deck smelled of furtive sunlight and old Benson & Hedges. It rumbled along an empty Allerton Road, where the McCartneys must have done their shopping, past the tangle of roads and roundabouts called the Maze and the trees of Queen's Drive; past the shops and the fab 1960s library where Michael McCartney read his books and dreamed about photography; past the fire station that may or may not be referred to in *Penny Lane*; on and on past sleeping supermarkets and open playing fields, more trees and thick slabs of semi-detached houses, a church and a synagogue. Then the bus stopped at the bus stop Paul and Michael would have used. I got off and crossed the empty road, drenched in birdsong and sunshine, and I was opposite Forthlin Road.

This is deep suburban Allerton, quiet and respectable. The first home Paul McCartney remembered was the house on Western Avenue in Speke but, since the National Trust acquired his last family home on Forthlin Road, Allerton has become reluctantly associated with the Beatles. When Paul and the family moved here it was a fairly new district, the older houses no more than 50 years old and most of the smaller ones only 20 or 30 years old. It is a suburb built for the motor car, a place of long, straight, landscaped roads and semi-detached houses with gardens and driveways. It is safe, decent, conservative and ferociously dull.

Smithdown Road, May 1961.

Paul's house, the old McCartney home, is a small, unobtrusive terraced house with a front garden, a modern terraced house very different from Ringo's home on Madryn Street or George's on Arnold Grove. It is on an estate of neat, suburban, ex-Corporation streets, built in the middle of the 20th century, with two-storey terraced houses and small blocks of Corporation flats on quiet streets generously laid out with gardens and safe places for children to play. They were full of sunshine and birdsong. A lawnmower hummed in the distance. Walking the streets in the early morning, the neighbours seemed mostly to be at work, but there was an old couple talking over the garden gate and a man trimming a hedge who stopped to look at me with friendly curiosity. They must be used to visitors here, the National Trust minibus pulling up and the old stories being rolled out once again. Jim and Mary McCartney's house is pin-sharp immaculate, the door freshly painted, the garden neat and respectable. Jim was a keen gardener and a member of the Speke Horticultural Society, planting snapdragons and dahlias in the garden and growing hedges of lavender, which he dried to burn in the house like incense to clear the rooms of the smell of tobacco smoke. Apart from writing *Penny Lane*, Paul is not associated with Allerton as John is with Woolton. His mother died when he was aged 14, but his childhood was warm and secure, full of aunties and uncles and family parties. Paul was able to build on this love and support to become a strong adult, with the confidence to be more interested in people than places.

Forthlin Road hasn't changed much in half a century. The houses are still tidy and well looked after, privately owned now with new extensions giving bigger kitchens, additional bedrooms and new white plastic porches. The gardens are often carefully paved over for more cars in the driveways, the Morris Minors and Austins of the 1950s replaced by Passats and Mondeos, the workmen's Comma vans replaced by Ford Transits. The chimneys are clean and unused, electricity and gas replacing the coal and smokes of the 1950s.

Mather Avenue.

I spent some time in the house on my visit, walking from room to room and immersing myself still further in stories and mood. I came to feel that the 1950s were somehow more real, more present, than the modern world. Absorbed in time and place and people, I watched Paul, guitar slung over his back, close the door of No. 20 and collect his bicycle from the alleyway – the 'jigger' or the 'entry' as we'd call it in Liverpool – before wheeling it out of the gate. I followed him slowly on foot, 50 odd years later, in time to see him swing on to his bicycle across Mather Avenue for the ride over the hill to John's house, crossing the traffic of the Avenue and turning up one of the roads opposite. Mather Avenue had woken up. It is one of the arteries of the city, busier now with cars, lorries, pedestrians and two schoolboys at the bus stop on their way to the Liverpool Institute. The roads on the other side of Mather Avenue, running up the slope towards Allerton Road, have not changed much in half a century. They are a slight step higher on the

Liverpool social scale than the Corporation houses of Forthlin Road, very definitely middle-class housing. As if reflecting this, the hill starts here, pulling up off Mather Avenue. They are semi-detached with small front gardens, sacrificed in some cases to provide more space for cars. Like Forthlin Road and roads all over the city, they are more likely to have PVC windows, more likely to have an extension or an enclosed porch, and definitely more likely to have one if not two cars parked outside. But the two roads, Moorcroft and Cleveley, remain middle-class and respectable and still have some of their stained glass and their slate roofs, and perhaps their views down towards the distant river. These are still quiet streets, filled during the day with birdsong and distant traffic noise. The figure on the bike pumps hard on these steep streets. Still way ahead of me, he pauses at the top of the road for a breather, steps off the pedals and checks the road. All these roads run up the hill to the quiet end of Allerton Road, a place of large houses and sandstone walls, not bars, shops and restaurants. This was a social step up again from Cleveley Road or Moorcroft Road, and the bright semi-detached houses

Allerton Road.

Allerton Manor, 2010.

are left behind. These Allerton Road houses are larger, detached and set in their own grounds, but they are uncertain and defensive, a road suddenly of CCTV and razor wire. The trees are bigger, heavier, older.

There was an abrupt change of mood here, of both landscape and atmosphere. The junction of Cleveley Road and Allerton Road was where McCartney's Allerton met Lennon's Woolton, where the neat sounds of suburbia met something darker and wilder. I was at a boundary between the smart and respectable suburbs and the large, semi-rural estates of the city's rich, who built here from the early 1800s onwards. The houses have largely gone, but they have left a very English landscape of small ruins that both teenage Beatles knew well: overgrown sandstone walls, chaotic and disordered, green with lichen and gently blackened with ancient falls of soot; the ruined houses of smooth Woolton sandstones, vacant Italianate windows, roofs open to the sky; slippery stone paths, studded with marble pebbles, drowned in dead leaves; stands of gigantic beech trees, trees that define this whole end of the city, smooth, silver-grey trunks like old elephants and rippled like warm muscle. This landscape is smothered with rhododendrons, giant flowers on pale spring mornings, and splashes of camellias like old dried blood. Distant traffic noises interrupt the strange silences. There is something wild and untamed hidden in these old parks, peering out at suburbia like a Green Man.

Paul's bicycle turns past the old lodge house and disappears into the greens, fairways and rough grass of Allerton Golf Course. This was the old entrance to Allerton Manor, the lodge house designed two centuries ago by Thomas Harrison (no relation). The club house has taken over the old stables for the Manor, and the course swept around the old house – now just a shell – and through the pleasure grounds laid out two centuries ago. There are stone staircases that lead nowhere and shallow pathways buried in wild shrubs, rediscovered as short-cuts by lazy golfers. Beech trees, planted perhaps by Harrison's ground staff to reach maturity today, stand in half-avenues defining the fall of the hill. This is

Fletcher's Farm track.

a wild place of neat fields – open country compared to the Allerton roads behind me.

Paul's bicycle carries him to the left of the old stable block and past the car park, and on the old lane to Fletcher's Farm. Immediately the landscape opens up, with the roofs of Woolton appearing over the brow of the hill and through the plantations of young trees. On this bright day I stopped here for a while, suddenly alone on the golf course, able to take some pictures and write notes. The mood was broken as a young lad on his way to school trailed over the fairway in front of me, giving the classic V-sign and some backchat to a man with a camera before disappearing as another group of golfers appeared from somewhere.

This was a favourite place for the McCartneys. Michael photographed George Harrison's new Jaguar car on the course in 1962, and in April 1963 Paul and the rest of the Beatles brought Dezo Hoffmann here for a photo shoot. Hoffmann was a professional photographer brought in by Brian Epstein to counter the surly 'bomb site' images taken by Les Chadwick, and to depict the Beatles as chirpy, lively and happy. He thought he was being taken to Sefton Park, but his Beatles leaping-in-the-air images were clearly taken on Allerton Golf Course. The key is the tiny skyline landmark, clearly the water tower on Reservoir Road in Woolton. The trees are still here, 50 years older, and the road still runs across to Fletcher's farm, but there is no plaque to mark this Beatles site, as there isn't one on the dock road. But to the bemusement of the golfers, I was able to goof around where the Beatles goofed around in 1963.

In an instant, as the sun goes behind a cloud and the land darkens, there is a change of mood, a blink of time, and an uncertain beam of torchlight. Julia Lennon sometimes had to take her two daughters, Julia and Jacqueline, to Mendips in the middle of the night across the darkened golf course when an angry, drunken Bobby Dykins had thrown them all out of the house on Blomfield Road, not far from Forthlin. But as the cloud passes, the sad image fades, the day is bright again and the golfers move on.

The rattle and whisky cheer of the golfers broke my mood and I remembered another old Liverpool myth, the story Kenny Everett told about taking LSD on this golf course with John Lennon in the early 1960s. The dates didn't connect, it didn't seem likely or even probable, but the thought of these two wild and creative men taking a trip among these greens and fairways made a great Liverpool drug culture story. In researching these places I found that it did happen but that it was Weybridge golf course, much later in the decade, which made more sense. And, of course, it was all done in the best possible taste.

Paul's bicycle was far ahead of me now. The farm track paused at the 18th-century Fletcher's Farm, the sandstone buildings converted to semi-rural urban homes, and then began a swift steep descent to the main road. The hedges were, oddly, wilder and less well-maintained, less groomed, perhaps trying to muffle the road noises from the golfers. The modern tower blocks of Woolton appeared on the other side of the road. The track stops abruptly at the four wide lanes of Menlove Avenue, another of the city's long artery roads, complete with trees and grass, tower blocks and a high wind. I am back in semi-detached suburbia, and this is the end of the walk. Paul slows his bicycle and stops here, just 100 yards or so from John's house on the other side of the road. This was Woolton suburbia, not Allerton suburbia, a social cut above where I had walked from. I watched Paul push his bicycle across the road and turned away into old Woolton, trying to imagine his face as Aunt Mimi calls up the stairs, 'John! Your little friend's here…'

John Lennon's Woolton

Childhood and landscape are sometimes, perhaps always, inextricably linked, connected by memory and geography of home, school and play. John Lennon's Woolton is a sprawling, shape-shifting place, beyond geographical boundaries and chronology, running from Allerton Road to Mendips to Reynolds Park to Newcastle Road; a landscape of childhood playgrounds, wild places, trees, sweet shops and bus stops, all with a sense of security as thin as a cigarette paper. It is a landscape of childhood, a landscape revisited physically, and in dreams and songs. It is a place of escape.

I grew up between the Stanley house on Newcastle Road and Lennon's home on Menlove Avenue, and of all these Beatles landscapes these are the most familiar to me. I knew the streets he grew up in, the parks, the shops in the village. Friends of mine went to his old school, still run by Lennon's headmaster, Mr Pobjoy, and still called Quarry Bank, at least unofficially. Names linger in Liverpool, and time moves slowly in her suburbs. The 1960s, the Beatles past, and even a more distant past of 1940s childhood seemed fluid, at one moment immediate and relevant, at others as distant as the Middle Ages.

There was a legend in the Stanley family that they had once owned all of Woolton, or

Quarry Bank High School building, 2010.

Menlove Avenue, 1936.

so John remembered. Perhaps this was a mish-mash of stories, a legend originating from Uncle George's family owning large areas of pasture land in and around the village and the more famous Stanley family, who were important Liverpool landowners. Woolton has been a suburb for less than 100 years, so when John lived here there would have been people who remembered the village before it was in Liverpool. It still feels

Rural Woolton, 2010.

rural, a very green suburb, bordered and defined by trees, the brick-and-sandstone village heart surrounded by large gardens, open fields and parkland.

There were still farms in Woolton and even Allerton when John was a boy. Until recently one of them had been run by the Smith family, but in the 1940s the fields were commandeered by the government for the war effort. Lennon's first home in Woolton was with his mother, Julia, in the old Dairy Cottage on Allerton Road (the other Allerton Road, there are two Allerton Roads and Woolton Roads within a mile or so of each other) which was attached to the farm house. The dairy business and farm was run by George Smith, who was married to John's Auntie Mimi. She wanted Julia to live there so they would be closer to her house and so they could also be out of the Stanley house on Newcastle Road, possibly because of their mother's illness. John lived with his mother in the cottage between 1942 and 1943, when he was a very small boy. It was presumably here that his mother fed him pastries for breakfast that she had been given in the pubs the night before when she was out drinking in Woolton Village. There is a story that she used to leave John asleep when she went out, and that the small boy would often wake alone and afraid in the dark house, the start of a life-long fear of abandonment and the dark. How did she sneak past the Smith family next door? In any case, they didn't stay long at the cottage. His mother was not cut out for parenthood and by the time he was five or six he was living permanently with George and Mimi.

John lived at Mendips for nearly half his life, and nowhere else is so closely associated with him. 'I was a nice, clean-cut suburban boy,' he said, 'and in the class system I was about a half an inch in a higher class than Paul, George and Ringo, who lived in subsidised government houses. We owned our own house, had our own garden. They didn't have anything like that.' The house was decent, respectable and middle-class with a large garden, which still feels secluded, with irises and fruit trees. Mimi was one of five sisters and Uncle George had seven siblings, so John was surrounded by an extended family of cousins, aunties and uncles.

George was the other side of the coin to Mimi. She showed love through convention and discipline, whereas George was softer, taking John up a comic and a chocolate bar when he had been sent to bed in disgrace. In the old photographs Mimi looks stern, smiling and on-duty; Uncle George looks a bit crumpled and uncertain. He was more physically affectionate towards the boy and always bathed him and put him to bed at night. He bought John his first harmonica and taught him to read from the *Liverpool Echo* headlines. Mimi sounds like the sort of woman who could smile and frown at the same time. When John first came to live with her and George in 1946, George's mother, Alice Smith, was still alive. She was the head of the Smith family in Woolton, perhaps living in the old family farmhouse, so perhaps it is not unreasonable to assume that John would have known the old lady, even that she might have become a distant surrogate grandmother after Mimi's mother had died in 1941 or 1945, depending on who's telling the story. George's brother Frank was still around as well, perhaps still in Woolton. The two brothers had run the family dairy business until the beginning of the war, when the dairy fields were requisitioned, although George still had a milk round and they possibly still had the dairy shop. Another one of the Smith brothers was George Harrison's English teacher at the Institute. I wonder if he taught Paul as well? Later Mimi's sister, Harriet, lived in Dairy Cottage with her husband,

Dairy Cottage Woolton, 2010.

Norman Birch, and their children David and Liela. Harriet was an interesting woman. In the mid-1930s she had been a student at the University of Liverpool, where she had met and married an Egyptian student called Ali Hafez. They went to live in Cairo but Ali died having a tooth out, so Harriet brought their daughter Liela home to Liverpool. The Stanley family was large, rambling and loving, and the Stanley cousins, John and Liela, and Stanley Parkes, used to go around Woolton on George's horse-drawn milk float, delivering milk from a large churn on the back.

Lennon's childhood was complicated, unpredictable and unsettled. Unable to cope with it at the time or to lose the memory since, he remembered Julia visiting Mendips after being beaten by John 'Bobby' Dykins, her face bleeding, and he seems to have turned up at Mendips many times in tears after Julia had left him with other sisters. Like Ritchie Starkey on Admiral Grove, he extended the good aspects of his family into his friendships, surrounding himself with a gang of schoolfriends whose childhood games and play turned eventually into music-making. The road behind Mendips, Vale Road, was where John's schoolboy gang, Nigel Whalley, Pete Shotton and Ivan Vaughan, known as 'the Outlaws', lived. This was John's first gang and first band, initially called the Outlaws before becoming Quarrymen. I heard a story once that John knew Ivan lived on Vale Road and just turned up on the doorstep in a heavy rainstorm one day, clutching a handful of Dinky toys, wanting to play. Likewise, Ritchie's friendship with Davey Patterson and Brian Briscoe set the mould for involvement with Dingle street gangs, the Hurricanes, the Beatles, and the All-Starr bands he tours with today.

On a fine sunny afternoon, with the light cooling, I walked from Mendips along Menlove Avenue to the junction with Yew Tree Lane and Beaconsfield Road, which turns tightly up the hill towards Quarry Street and Woolton Village. Beaconsfield Road is a busy, narrow road – an old country lane swamped and baffled by the suburbs, like many of the smaller roads in this area – with high walls of sandstone and very little room for pedestrians. Thick forest trees towered over the sandstone walls, hiding the large old houses behind them. Some houses had been converted into apartments, some reused as schools, and others surprised me by being idle and derelict, with wild overgrown gardens, but the most famous of these old houses had already gone. Strawberry Field was built in the late 19th century and became a Salvation Army children's home in 1934. John Lennon walked up Beaconsfield Road to Strawberry Field many times and famously used to tug at Mimi's sleeve when he heard the band strike up at a garden party, 'Mimi, come on, we're going to be late…' He played here with Pete Shotton and Ivan Vaughan, running wild in the wooded grounds of the old house. In the 1950s the grounds of Strawberry Field ran alongside Beaconsfield Road down to Mather Avenue, before a small number of houses were built at the bottom, so the woods were far bigger in those days.

Even today Woolton has many decaying parks and big houses, and I found it difficult not to imagine the young John Lennon, rebellious,

Strawberry Fields gates, 2010.

insecure and curious, roaring through these wild woods, first to play Pirates or Cowboys and Indians; then to make camp fires and smoke; and later to read, drink and try and have sex. I saw them as a background to his life at Mendips, the antithesis of Mimi's neatness and desire to control, perhaps even as an early form of rock 'n' roll, the wild side of nature. Is it a coincidence that Paul McCartney's Beatles songs seemed to look out into the world whereas John Lennon's work was darker, wilder, more introspective?

Strawberry Fields Forever brought together the strange worlds of childhood and psychedelic word play. The house seems to have been a tall, rather gloomy building, with a spiky roofline and lots of chimneys. The Salvation Army ran it as a family home, and many of the children came back with happy memories of living there in the 1970s and 1980s. The old house that John Lennon would have remembered was demolished in the early 1970s and replaced by smaller, more intimate buildings that the Salvation Army called John Lennon Court. Strawberry Field is no longer a children's home and is run by the Salvation Army as a prayer centre and artists' studios, a strange echo of other aspects of his life.

I could just about see the workshops and quiet places of John Lennon Court through the thick tangle of greenery that surrounds the new buildings and guards their privacy, for, of course, Strawberry Field is a Beatles site, and the gates of the old house – which survived the demolition and still stand today – get thousands of visitors on the Beatles trail. It is a curve of wall, two undistinguished stone gateposts and a typically Victorian sweep of wrought iron gate painted bright red, but it has become a rock 'n' roll shrine, famous and identifiable all over the world. Like all good rock 'n' roll shrines it is covered in messages and graffiti from fans and visitors. The gates are repainted and cleaned every now and then, but the messages return, marks of gentle hippie pilgrimage, to be photographed thousands, if not millions, of times. The internet has countless pages of images of the gates, pictures of visitors from America, Spain, Germany or Japan standing self-consciously next to the pillars and the old ironwork, and those magical words 'Strawberry Field'. For years, before the city took control of the Beatles industry and started celebrating these places, the gates were only occasionally visited and (with the big house demolished) were an object of idle curiosity and a focus of reminiscence. I have walked past them many times, and seen them in many moods and weathers. In bright sunshine – which is rare, because they are so shaded – the gates look cheerful and fresh, even though the path behind clearly leads nowhere. But on autumn afternoons, as the light starts to fade in the trees, there is a gentle melancholy to the gates, as if they too remember past glories. I stood alone at the gates in the thin sunshine, reading the messages and thinking that for all the fresh paint the gates looked old and careworn, and they resembled many other redundant gateways in the city, entrances to grand Liverpool houses no longer there. The driveway beyond was gently silted with drifts of crisp leaves like the fall of years, which added to my mood of soft gloom. But then another coachload of excited visitors arrived and the noisy traffic built up again, and my mood was broken.

Beaconsfield Road took me up the hill beneath the trees. There were thick forest trees everywhere, large, mature trees, chestnut, oak and above all beech. Woolton seemed as thickly wooded, if not more so, than it was 50 years ago. The old houses have left a legacy of

Beech trees, Reynolds Park, 2010.

sandstone walls – from the many quarries in the area, 'quarry men' could almost be a Woolton nickname. Dark red sandstone and beech trees defined the whole of this part of south Liverpool. I was heading for Reynolds Park along roads and pavements, but I could see the young John Lennon leading the Outlaws – faces painted, feathers and leaves in their hair – across the old estates instead of around them, scrambling over walls and through thick woodland to find a longer and more interesting short cut, leaving behind a melee of barking dogs and angry residents waving their fists at them.

At the busy crossroads at the top of the hill the view opened suddenly, with panoramic views down Blackwood Avenue towards Prescot and Huyton. A shaved lawn of beech trees runs down the middle of the Avenue, their muscular trunks tall and proud. This is an old junction with roads coming from Allerton, Woolton Village, Gateacre and Woolton Road, busy but awkward to use, as if the junction was there for the convenience of the roads not the convenience of travellers. I turned right onto Church Road, the old route to Woolton Village. A couple of hundred yards of mature trees are hidden behind sandstone walls, and with a crash and a roar of old leaves and curses, the gang of wild boys jumped over the wall and ran across the road without looking, shrieking and waving sticks, swords, cutlasses, pistols. They disappeared into the quiet wilderness of Reynolds Park, their voices fading. The entrance is small and discreet, and had I blinked I would have missed it. This is the most hidden of Liverpool's parks, the most peaceful and perhaps the most

Woolton Road.

Reynolds Park, 2010.

beautiful of the city's green secrets. Like many city parks it was once an estate, but the big house here disappeared only a few years ago. It is not a big park and can be walked around in five minutes, but I had the time and Reynolds Park revealed a strange tension, a strange pull of opposites. There were the usual civic amenities, display boards of park history, bins and tarmac paths, but I could hear the boys clattering and fighting in the dark rhododendron thickets and caught distant sight of them on broken paths lined with gigantic, muscular beech trees. Old sandstone garden or landscape features, disturbed by tree roots, reared out of the path or disappeared into the undergrowth, and the park seemed sliced by hedges and ha-has. There are strange half-circles of bricks in the path, the ruins of small buildings razed to the ground, and yet the park is dominated by bright lawns and carefully clipped formal gardens. It is a landscape divided by light and shade, especially as the summer advances and the leaves thicken on the trees. John Lennon came here in the first rush of anger and despair when Julia was killed in the summer of 1958, with on-off girlfriend Barbara Baker, hugging her and

Church Road, Woolton.

crying his heart out in his grief and bewilderment. His pain still resonates here for Beatles walkers, for all its beauty, and Lennon's childhood is still difficult to read about today. I could no longer hear the boys playing.

Church Road took me thoughtfully into Woolton Village, past Reservoir Road with its distinctive water tower. I thought of the golf course across Menlove Avenue and Dezo Hoffmann's famous 1963 *Twist and Shout* photograph of the Beatles in mid-air. The tower is surrounded by respectable 1920s middle-class houses, like Mendips away over the hill. Further on, the road starts to drop steeply into Woolton Village and back onto the Beatles pilgrimage trail. Church Road runs between two of the most famous places associated with the Beatles in Liverpool, St Peter's Church and the church hall, and even on this cool sunny day there were small groups of fans taking photographs. Aunt Mimi attended services regularly at St Peter's, though it didn't surprise me to read

St Peter's Church.

St Peter's church hall.

that John was a reluctant churchgoer – it is said that he was so bored by services that he used to count the panes of stained glass in the windows – but he sang in the choir here and was a member of the youth club for a time, which is how the Quarrymen were offered the church fête gig in 1957. The church hall across the road is still the same building where John met Paul in 1957, and their meeting is marked by a plaque on the wall. The story is well known – the introduction by Ivan Vaughan, Paul's ability to play *Twenty Flight Rock* and remember the words and Pete Shotton's invitation to join the band some weeks later as Paul was cycling through the village; where was he going, I wonder? Julia and Mimi also heard John play and sing with the band for the first time on that July day. Mimi gave two versions of her reaction – she was 'pleased as Punch' to see him doing so well and also horrified to see him up there on stage. Astonishingly, a recording of the band playing that day has survived, a fraction of musical memory, conveying the sounds that Mimi, Juli and Paul heard when they watched the Quarrymen here for the first time: a Woolton memory from the Church Fete of 1957.

Woolton is a green urban village, fashionable and popular, but there are moments of Lennon darkness here as well, reflecting John's unsettled childhood. He was 14 years old when Uncle George died suddenly, aged

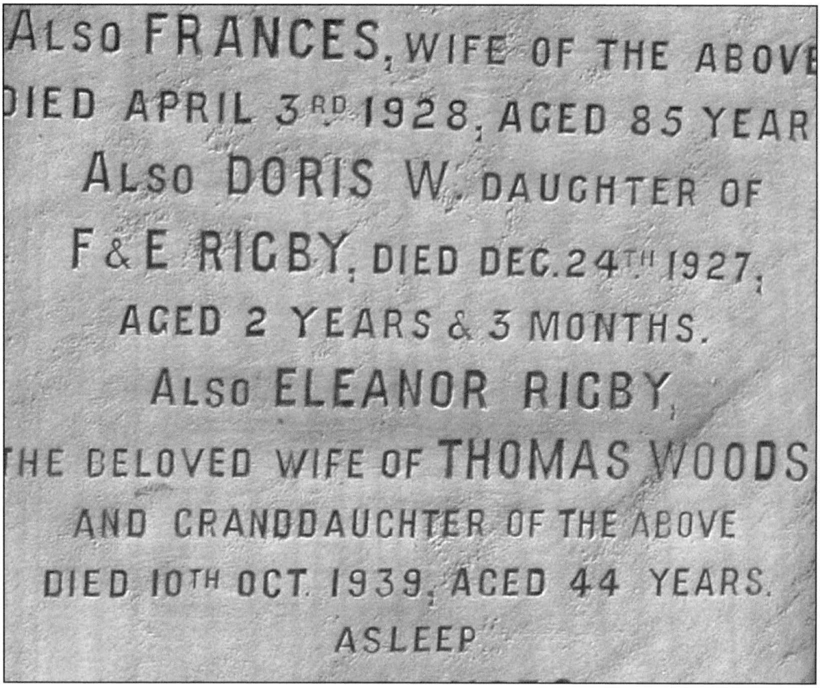

Eleanor Rigby's grave.

only 52, and John was devastated. George Smith is buried in a family grave in St Peter's, tucked away from Beatles visitors behind the church. Lennon inherited George's overcoat and wore it constantly during his years as an art student, clinging to presence, memory and comfort. The churchyard around St Peter's was full of Woolton stories, names and places. There was at least one Dykins grave here as well, relatives perhaps of Julia's second partner, John Dykins. Julia called him Bobby as there was already a John in her life; less sentimentally, John called him Twitchy. But most fans were here to photograph the most famous grave, which partly belongs to Eleanor Rigby.

As Liverpool's definitive urban village, Woolton is more fashionable than when John lived here, but physically the centre hasn't changed much. The streets are narrow and feel cramped, reflecting the rural working-class village – with a pub on every corner – that Woolton used to be. There is no sense of the fields and woods around the village; it is easier to see into than out of. And there are more cars – there are more cars everywhere – but the buildings haven't really changed since the 1950s. Church Road runs down to the crossroads by the old drovers' pond, now a car park surrounded by trees. There are large supermarkets here now (very well hidden), but the smaller shops seem to have survived, and in the 1950s this would have been where the family did their weekly shopping, so John would have known the shops of Woolton well. An old-fashioned range of butchers and bakers has been kept, alongside the estate agents and charity shops. I imagine he knew the pubs too, although probably not with Aunt Mimi. These may have been the places his mother drank in during that lonely winter of 1942 – the Grapes, the Elephant, the White Horse and the Coffee House. The Quarrymen played Woolton Village Club one night in January 1959, which hasn't changed externally since the band left. But wandering around the village I felt that the wild spaces of Woolton would hold more appeal than the shops.

Uncle George used to go off for the day with John, leaving only a note for Mimi. Perhaps away from Mimi's conventionality, George was the sort of person who would cut across fields and through woods – and he'd know the Woolton fields and woods very well – and so show the young John old dens and hidey-holes from his childhood, setting the tone for John's explorations with the Outlaws. He certainly often used to take him to the park. Another journey from Mendips took me across the junction with Beaconsfield Road to Calderstones Park, 94 acres of fields and lakes and woodland, the second-biggest park in the city. Lennon often used to cycle to school, and his route would take him from Mendips across Menlove Avenue to Yew Tree Lane and into Calderstones Park, probably over the low wall. Like Ringo, John had a number of routes to school. If the weather was good and he had plenty of time, he could walk up over the golf course, past Fletcher's Farm, the route that would later take him to Forthlin Road; but instead of walking all the way

John's route to school – the Mansion House and Linda McCartney playground, Calderstones Park.

into Allerton, he could turn off at any point and walk across the course to the narrow footpath to Calderstones Park, a quiet, peaceful route away from traffic and people.

Calderstones was John's favourite city park, and he is supposed to have bought Tittenhurst Park in Surrey because it reminded him of here. It is nothing like the overgrown thickets and rhododendron glades of the abandoned big houses, the old quiet places of Woolton and Allerton. It is a well-managed park of winding footpaths and carriageways, open fields, a lake, and careful plantations of large mature trees. The park was laid out to be seen

The lake, Calderstones Park.

and to be experienced from the big house, built in 1828 and known as the Mansion House. Still the centre and focus of the park, like a little bit of white-stucco-Georgian London dropped into the city, it has a small café and has been used as council offices for many years. The old outbuildings – stables and workshops – are also still here, now also used by the council. For many years the council's horses were stabled here.

In half a century this landscape has changed very little. The trees are taller and more mature, and no doubt some have been lost to storms. The boathouse on the lake has gone, which caters now more for anglers than pleasure boats. Calderstones Park's tennis courts have been restored and developed and now hold Liverpool's international tennis competition every summer, one of the biggest in the north of England. A children's playground was opened recently by Paul McCartney and dedicated to his late wife, Linda. The park is connected to the golf course at Allerton by a country footpath, and the green space here runs all the way to Hunts Cross. Paul McCartney also knew these fields as a boy.

Perhaps Paul also attended concerts at the open-air theatre in Calderstones Park, as John was supposed to have done, according to the popular myth from my childhood. Perhaps this is local mingling of the famous story that he went with Mimi to concerts at Strawberry Field, but with Mimi's aspirational interest in culture it is not impossible and not too unlikely. It is the nearest theatre venue to Mendips and would have run concerts and events in many of the summer months, as it did in the late 1960s when I attended them.

John Lennon's bicycle would have carried him at some speed from Yew Tree Lane to Harthill Road along the wide carriageways in the park, through a landscape he would still recognize. One large change is that the neighbouring estate of Harthill no longer has the city's botanic gardens, long lines of greenhouses with exotic lilies and rare orchids. This disappeared in the troubled 1980s but was probably of little interest to the teenage Lennon. The Old English Garden and the Japanese Garden around the Mansion House are still well-maintained,

Calderstones open-air theatre, 1958.

Four Seasons gates, Harthill.

and the smaller rose and other gardens have been developed and extended. And the Calder Stones themselves, the oldest man-made structure in Liverpool, still stand silently behind protective plastic glass, a Neolithic burial chamber reduced to its giant component pieces. His bicycle would have whizzed past them.

John would have passed from the Calderstones estate to the Harthill estate and emerged onto Harthill Road through the magnificent set of gates that at one time marked the entrance to Harthill (in plenty of time for a cigarette before school started.) These gates are known informally as the 'four seasons gates' because of the allegorical figures of girls and women representing the four seasons on the low wall around them. They are life-sized, well-carved, still strong after a 150 years of Liverpool weathers. John regularly used this wall – and probably these statues – as a stage to amuse, infuriate and harangue his fellow pupils.

I stood invisible under the beech trees near the gates as the school bell sounded in 1956 and the muttering, laughing crowd of children stamped out their cigarettes and wheeled their bicycles slowly through the school gates on Harthill Road. The park was once more quiet and sunny behind me. Perhaps because they were all boys, I felt that green open space played a huge role in the lives of all four Beatles, from Paul and George wandering for miles along the shore at Oglet and Dungeon Lane, to John exploring Reynolds Park, Strawberry Field and Calderstones Park. Ringo is the most built-up and urban Beatle, but even he remembered going to school through Princes Park and going to fairs in the enormous Sefton Park from the tight streets around High Park Street. I turned away to walk along Menlove Avenue. Woolton meant a lot to John Lennon and thoughts of the village and his childhood landscapes stayed with him into adulthood, so much so that one quiet day in the 1970s, out shopping in the village, a friend of mine was surprised to see John Lennon and Yoko Ono walking through the village alone, without bodyguards or assistants. He was pointing out to her the places he remembered from his childhood.

Moondogs in Bohemia

There is an old Liverpool story that the shadow of the Anglican Cathedral is somehow haunted, that it holds a deeper darkness within it, a place of strange happenings and dark events. There are odd folk memories here of an ancient village not on any maps that supposedly once stood on St James's Mount, which once held a statue of the child-eating witch, Jenny Greenteeth, a memory of dark things released as the foundations for the Christian building were being dug. For all its beauty, this is a strange part of the city, a watchful place, Liverpool's bohemia – a studenty, boozy, foodie area squeezed between cathedrals, Chinatown, Liverpool 8 and the universities. When John and Stuart were at the art college and George and Paul were at the Institute, the Quarrymen were growing up, flexing their muscles, looking out from the suburbs and into the exciting, unsettling city. 'Me and George Harrison didn't do well at school, but you had to go and you had to take exams, whether you

The Art College and the Institute.

The Liverpool Institute.

Bohemia.

passed or not,' said Paul. 'John didn't do at all well at school, and he didn't do an awful lot at art school. He was not a keen painter, but this is where we were coming from and this is why it all happened.'

After getting off the No. 82 bus from Speke on Berry Street, as George and Paul would have done, I climbed towards the shadow, through the steep grid of streets up from Berry Street and the bombed-out church of St Luke's. It is a noisy, muscle-pulling hike up Duke Street or Hardman Street, out and up from the city centre. I chose the quieter route up Knight Street and Mount Street, through Chinatown with its otherworldly smells of salt and tea and gunpowder, a place of dusty car parks, graffiti-walls and bricked up windows. I was struck by the pace of change in the city and how it flowed like water, sometimes fast, sometimes slow. New businesses had swept over old workshops, garages and overgrown gardens, but I could still hear birds in hidden trees and the greasy smokers' yards of restaurants. Gradually, quietly, the city slipped away behind me, and the river appeared as a distant silver streak. Laughter and a smell of beer escaped from the Grapes pub, tucked away on the corner of Roscoe Street. I was tempted by memories of chance drinking sessions and bags of books, afternoons of beer and sunlight on the scuffed wooden floor; but Beatles stories pulled me up the hill, past beautiful, mad, unloved Roscoe Street, a boundary between city centre commercial and city centre residential, a book in itself. Distant traffic can be heard from Rodney Street between dark, high brick walls. Rodney Street is brash and busy, over-confident and self-important, like a London street, but for Liverpool it *is* important, a street of consultant dentists and private doctors, exclusive clinics and hidden consulates. It has an air of confidence, sophistication and worldliness. Brian Epstein was born here, in a private nursing home, in 1934.

The road still climbing, as Knight Street becomes Mount Street, I remembered a faint Beatles link, a recorded story, another connection with Brian Epstein. In early 1962 John Lennon's friend, Ian Sharp, told him that Epstein was gay, and Sharp promptly received a stiff letter from

Bohemia.

Brian's solicitor – would this be Rex Makin? – who demanded an apology and a formal recantation. Sharp was walking up Mount Street a few days later when a taxi full of girls and Beatles hailed him and an apologetic Lennon shouted across that they had signed an agreement with Brian never to speak to Ian Sharp again. The 1960s cab roared off up the street, taking the Beatles back towards Hamburg, fame and fortune. Above Pilgrim Street – an uncertain half-connection between the cathedrals – I looked up at tall Mount Street houses with their brick walls and white windows, and bright Georgian doors. Dignified and graceful, their three storeys are draped in roses or wisteria and black iron railings guard mysterious cellars. I slipped into bohemia.

I had crossed an invisible city boundary, from the regular city into the cathedral's shadow. Bohemia is a state of mind, an idea, an invisible place of acceptance for artists and poets, oddballs and low-lifes, where academia and the literary world rub shoulders with crime and alcoholism. There is a physical bohemia too, a geography of creativity – bars and restaurants, studios, galleries and music venues, where artists meet other artists, eat cheaply, drink all night, argue with passion and wake up in cold-water flats with the rain on the windows. In the old city's pubs, perhaps an Irish legacy, artists are usually respected, writers are valued and creativity is understood as an ideal. Liverpool's bohemia is scattered across the south end of the city, in the old residential roads around Catherine Street, Smithdown Road, Belvidere Road, Lark Lane and Sefton Park, cheap areas of students and writers, poets, painters and musicians. Here on Hope Street, a maze of old streets has been reborn for the solicitors and bankers who can afford these houses, places brought back from neglect surrounded by new bars, chic hotels and restaurants. Hope Street and Falkner Street smell of warm breads, Gauloise and garlic butter. The bohemian city centre is and was a loose, ever-changing swirl of clubs and pubs spiralling drunkenly out from the two centres of student activity, the University of Liverpool and, more importantly, the Liverpool College of Art.

Mount Street brought me back onto the Beatles' trail at the art college and the old Liverpool Institute. John Lennon started at the art college in the autumn of 1957, not long after meeting Paul McCartney at the St Peter's Church fête. Paul was already studying at the Institute, with George a year or two below him. I was firmly back on the Beatles' trail here, back in the Beatles legends, old stories repeated and reheated of John Lennon and Stuart Sutcliffe at the art college where Paul and George would join them from school next door, slipping through a gap in the fence into a different world. There were impromptu lunchtime rehearsals, short canteen performances, and impressions of Lennon skitting through the college on a wing and a prayer, skiving classes – better than working. He found college life stiflingly dull, but he also found a different world at art college, a world of people – Stuart, Cynthia, Bill Harry – who were giving themselves to a life infused with art, writing, journalism and painting. And for the first time he plunged into the artistic world that fed the college and was fed by it himself, through the artists around the streets and the city's bohemia. Lennon took far more readily to this artistic world, this demi-monde, of afternoon drinking sessions and endless conversations about art, poetry and books. It was a world in perpetual twilight to the outside world, a place of decaying, gloomy streets and unconventional hours, hidden in plain view behind the grand façades of Hope Street – a very long way from Menlove Avenue.

Much of the physical bohemian landscape is still here as they left it half a century ago. The art college still stands next to the Liverpool Institute, and I sat on a street sculpture of suitcases to look at the two buildings, wildly different in style and taste. Here, on Mount Street and Hope Street, McCartney still meets Lennon every day; hard work and Georgian dignity rubs shoulders with Edwardian Baroque.

Hope Street was once open countryside, the houses of merchants on the ridge looking down on the smokes of the old town below. It is famous in the city today for connecting the two cathedrals, a metaphor

Ye Crake, Rice Street.

of Hope connecting Catholic and Protestant. Between these two, older bohemianism has ossified into the great cultural institutions of Liverpool – the Philharmonic Hall, LIPA, the Everyman Theatre, the Unity Theatre, the Philharmonic pub. Hope Street has not changed much in the last 50 years, though it is more fashionable now with new restaurants and bars appearing to cater to the bankers and solicitors. Yet it seems a place of great buildings slightly come down in the world.

I turned a few yards along Hope Street – if I had blinked I would have missed it – onto Rice Street, a short, narrow street squeezed between the grand buildings of Hope Street and the workshops and garages of Pilgrim Street. The street was once far poorer. The saddest thing on Rice Street is the sign, overpainted, ignored and almost invisible, screwed to the wall of the pub, which reads 'COURT NO 1'. Ye Cracke is an old pub by Liverpool standards, the only survivor of a street of courts – cramped, unhygienic and overcrowded houses that were thrown up across the city in the 19th century, a dark link with Saltney Street and Great Homer Street. Once a Welsh boozer called the Ruthin Castle, it is another stop on the Beatles' trail, the number one Beatles pub in the city. I have drunk here many times and have lost snug winter evenings in the War Office or listening to a blues band in the big room and lazy summer afternoons in the concrete beer garden – beer yard – outside. John Lennon and Stuart Sutcliffe were regulars at Ye Cracke, where they would drink Black Velvets – a mixture of Guinness and champagne, or more commonly cider – at lunchtime. Ye Cracke is a small, scruffy, knockabout pub, a pub of corridors pretending to be rooms, tiny, narrow ledges and leaded windows. For some reason the War Office, the smallest public room in the pub (even the toilets are bigger), is the only listed part of the whole building. This is still a student pub, an artists' pub, with rough wooden floors and plain walls, wearing its Beatles legacy lightly, like an uncle's overcoat thrown around his shoulders. It is a busy and crowded, spit-and-sawdust alehouse with drinkers standing shoulder-to-shoulder. And, as pubs will, it has collected stories and myths. There is a story that John and Paul once sang in the War Office of an afternoon to entertain the drinkers, perhaps passing the hat. A more reliable one states that John Lennon brought Cynthia here after meeting her at the college dance. One of his art teachers once said that Lennon was 'a man born without brakes', the sort of penniless scruff-bag artist and rocker that turned one afternoon pint into a back-street pub crawl between opening hours. They call it 'lunchtime drinking' or 'enjoying a quiet pint', but I can see Lennon drinking all afternoon and on into the evening, drinking until he fell over or the money ran out, until there was nobody left to scrounge a pint from. After a few lunchtime beers he is said to have 'swam' in spilt beer on the floor. More unhappily, he is supposed to have drunk in Ye Cracke when he learned his mother, Julia, had been killed in the summer of 1958. 'I was pretty self-destructive at college,' he said later. 'I was a drunk and smashed phone boxes.'

I imagined that the art students drank in all the local pubs, as they still do – the Philharmonic, the Belvedere on tiny, amputated Sugnall Street, the Caledonian and the Blackburn Arms over on Catherine Street. Many of John's lunchtime drinkers would stagger home as the pubs opened again to flats on the residential Georgian streets behind Gambier Terrace and Hope Street – Falkner, Canning and Huskisson Streets, Falkner Square, and out towards Upper Parliament Street and Princes Avenue. Artists and students, living where the rent was cheap, on wide, gloomy streets of grand houses, soot-stained, unfashionable and scruffy, in the heart of Liverpool's red light district. In the 1950s and 1960s these old streets were rundown and neglected, the rich long gone and the houses bought cheaply and knocked into flats. The area of Georgian houses was much bigger, crossing Grove Street and running along Upper Parliament Street to Aigburth Street and Smithdown Lane, leaving a great ghost footprint of lost Georgiana. At Grove Street today the Georgian world ends abruptly, the amputated arms of Upper Huskisson and Upper Canning Streets reaching silently towards the grounds of the new women's hospital.

Some streets remain – in a city with more Georgian buildings than Bath, as the old improbable story has it – obscurity, insecurity, danger and dubious location all having preserved them. This area of the city – now fashionably called the Georgian Quarter – is cleaner than it was 100 years ago, an urban landscape defined by iron lamp posts, sandstone flagstones worn smooth and almost soft, black iron railings and ornamental balconies. The granite kerbstones and cobbles have been mended in case the streets are needed for a new TV show or film. But this is still Liverpool's red light district and these can be rough streets. There seems an air of unpredictability about them, a vague sensation of breaths being held to see what will happen next, a silence before a storm.

I walked away from Catherine Street and Hope Street to where the streets seemed to get quieter, like water slowing and calming away from the main stream. Canning Street was quieter than Hope Street, and Percy Street was quieter again, a street of beautiful pale sandstone terraces with basements and black ironwork. In Liverpool, only the churches can be relied on to be Gothic, but on Percy Street even the church, St Bride's, is classical in design, like a Greek temple. Percy Street is a five-minute walk from the art college, and there are still relatively low-rent properties in the street, although not many students could afford to buy a property here today. In 1959 Stuart Sutcliffe rented a flat at No. 9 Percy Street with art college classmate and best friend Rod Murray. Stuart was part of the new world that John found at the art college, a romantic, beautiful and

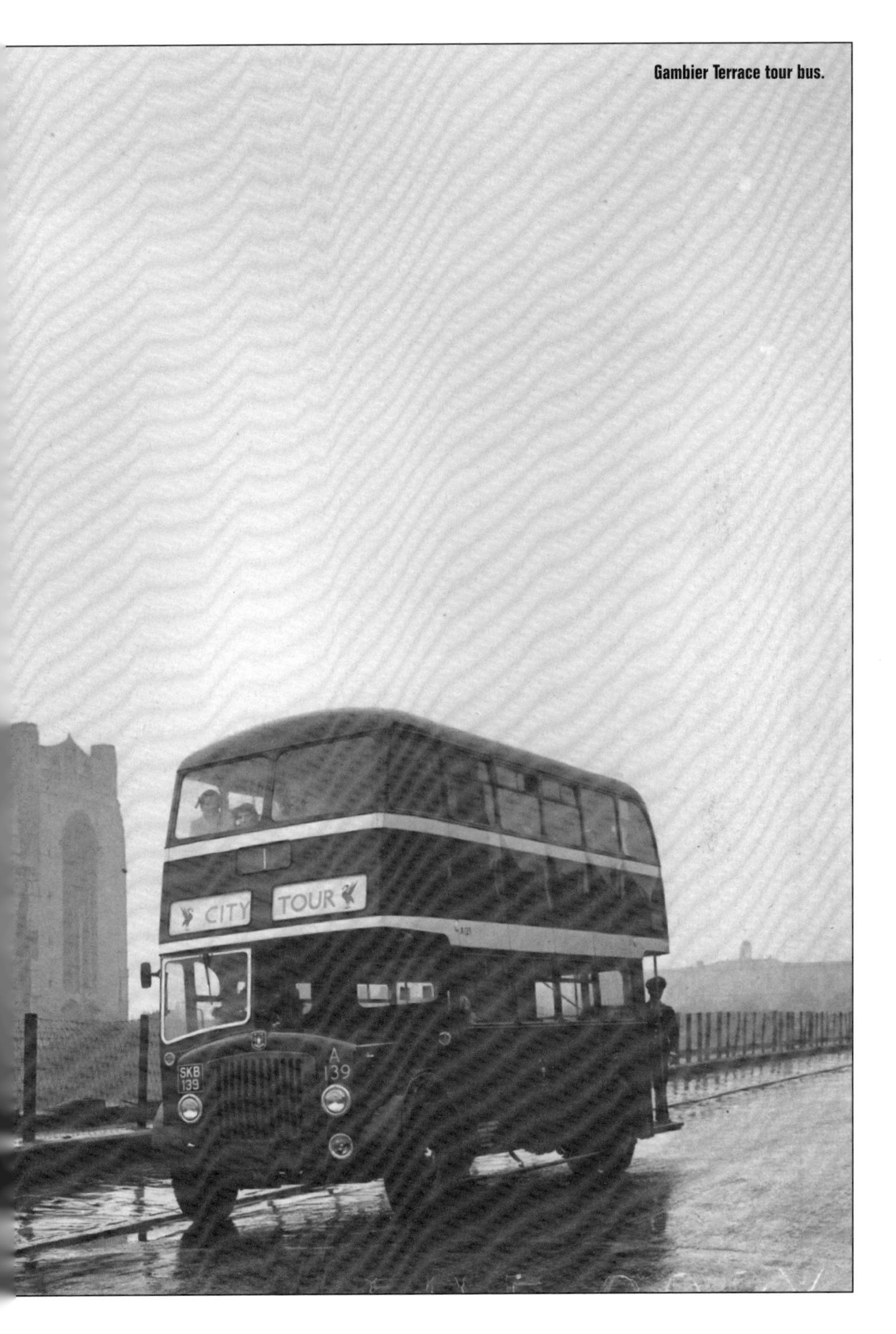

Gambier Terrace tour bus.

talented artist besotted with art, painting, rock 'n' roll and even, it has been said, with an early death. There were never any Moondogs in bohemia, but this was a time of hope, flux and name changes, from Silver Beatles and Silver Beetles and back again, Stuart managing them then Allan Williams finding their gigs. Paul remembered, 'one April evening in 1960, walking along Gambier Terrace, by Liverpool Cathedral, John and Stuart announced "Hey, we want to call the band The Beatles,"' just one of a hundred suggestions, memories and moments on the road to the famous name.

John was a frequent visitor to the Percy Street flat, and there is an old Liverpool myth that after one all-night party he climbed up onto the roof of the house to watch the sun rise and painted it on the low parapet wall in front of him. Percy Street is terraced, though, and the painting was done on a wall connecting two properties, so ownership of it has always been disputed,

No. 3 Gambier Terrace.

Gambier Terrace.

allowing this John Lennon original artwork to fade and wash away in the Liverpool rains. I once emailed *Mersey Beat* giant Bill Harry about this, and he told me that the story was largely a myth and that the painting certainly wasn't done by Lennon. But climbing up onto the slates after an all-night party seems a very John Lennon thing to do, and because it is not unimaginable the story stuck. Wandering alone along Percy Street, I wondered if it was still there.

The all-night parties – and burning the landlady's furniture to keep warm – contributed to Stuart and Rod's eviction from the flat in Percy Street in 1959 or early 1960. They moved to a flat on Gambier Terrace, flat three in a block called Hillary Mansions, for a rent of £3 a week. I paused on Percy Street and looked up at the backs of Gambier Terrace, wondering if I could see Stuart's room and thinking about cigarette smoke, painters' oils and a light burning at night. The moment passed with a burst of laughter as the students hauled their gear out of the Percy Street house. I followed their footsteps from Percy Street onto the grander but more formal Canning Street and round the corner to Gambier Terrace. I could see the laughing and excited students pushing their belongings on a hand cart, the wooden wheels and iron tyres clattering and slithering on the cobbles, the barrow piled with saggy mattresses, bags of clothes, canvases, tubes of paint and even an easel or two. Nobody uses the name 'Hillary Mansions' any more – like many names of Liverpool houses it has fallen into disuse and has been replaced by simple street numbers – but the flat was at No. 3 Gambier Terrace. The flat was up a long flight of stairs and ran the full length of the building. They painted the walls black and yellow and decorated it sparsely, although Pauline Sutcliffe and Bill Harry didn't remember it as too scruffy. As student places tend to be, there seems to have been a floating population in this flat. Stuart and Rod were joined by other art students and girlfriends, overnighters, people who'd spent their money on beer and missed the last bus. Even the bathroom was pressed into service as sleeping space when they had a party. John stayed there when he wasn't talking to Mimi – often sleeping in a silk-lined coffin, so the story goes – and later used to stay in Stuart's room with Cynthia. I once knew a man who lived in a neighbouring flat and who claimed to have burgled Stuart's flat when Lennon was living there, but other people remember the flat as very bare, with mattresses on the floor and half-used tubes of paint everywhere – it hardly sounds worth burgling! Stuart's room in particular sounds like a studio he could sleep in.

One day in early 1960, while drinking in the Jacaranda, Stuart met Royston Ellis. I liked the idea of Stuart Sutcliffe enjoying a quiet pint away from the crowds, music and the art students and bumping into 'the king of the beatniks'. At only 18 years old, Ellis had published two volumes of poetry and wrote a column for the *Record Mirror*. He was in Liverpool to give a poetry reading at the Jacaranda and persuaded Sutcliffe and the band to back him during his performance. He ended up staying at the Gambier Terrace flat for a week, introducing Stuart and John to Benzedrine from a Vicks inhaler and telling them all sorts of wicked stories about the London bohemia of gays and drugs to pay his way. In a very jazz-1950s-beatnik kind of way, Ellis lived in a blurred world between pop music, poetry, nightclubs and performance. Their age but a grown-up bohemian from London, they listened to him – I could almost hear John's sceptical awe – and in return he took their world seriously. Rock 'n' roll was as serious as literature, as serious as painting or poetry or free jazz. Ellis seems to have touched a nerve in John and to have been inspirational

Gambier Terrace from St James' Cemetery.

in convincing him to follow his dream and become the artist he should be, perhaps the poet, the writer. He encouraged him to work hard and to take the band seriously. After all, by then they had toured Scotland with Johnny Gentle. Reading this story, it occurred to me that of course Royston Ellis could have had the same impact on Stuart and so planted the seed of him leaving the bass guitar behind forever.

The Gambier Terrace flat is also infamous for the *Sunday People* article of July 1960. The newspaper ran a series of articles exposing beatnik

St James' Cemetery, 2010, as it must have looked in the early 1960s.

teenagers as drop-outs, malcontents on the road to ruin, living in filthy, drug-addled squalor. Bill Harry described these articles as 'a calculated, fabricated series to demonise young people'. Journalists used to drink in the Jacaranda so met Allan Williams, who agreed to set up some sort of photo-shoot for the journalists. In turn he seems to have had no problem getting Stuart, John and Rod Murray to trash their already-basic flat – or possibly the one below – for the journalists. 'The flat was roomy and sparse, lacking much furniture, and it wasn't seedy,' wrote Bill Harry, 'but it didn't take long for Williams and the *People* reporter and photographer to make it look scruffy, placing empty beer bottles on the floor, rumpling up old newspapers and scattering them about, making the furniture askew and generally turning the flat into a messy place.' Young people were photographed sitting about, rather politely, as if listening to a record and waiting for afternoon tea rather than their drug dealer. One of them was John Lennon, stretched out on the floor. The staged photograph and article was front-page news in the *People* on 24 July 1960. Did John arrange for a copy to be delivered to Mendips? I could all too easily imagine a gleeful John rushing back to Menlove Avenue and waving the paper at Mimi, just as I could easily imagine Mimi's reaction.

Gambier Terrace sits overlooking the giant Anglican Cathedral, which was in the long process of being built when

36 Falkner Street.

Falkner Street.

Lennon and Sutcliffe lived there. Over Hope Street and beyond the railings is a deep chasm, St James's Cemetery, originally a quarry whose stone was used for many of Liverpool's town-centre buildings. Another Liverpool quarry, another bunch of Quarrymen! In 1960 the cemetery was wildly overgrown, with tombstones buried beneath greenery or standing tall of thick foliage. I could easily imagine the young John Lennon being fascinated by this romantic, hidden and overgrown landscape, but I have no evidence that he ever explored this space, which is strangely reminiscent of the overgrown parks of Woolton. Artists have repeatedly imagined the Beatles in a soot-blackened and empty city or depicted them by derelict churches or overgrown cemeteries, and the abandoned graveyard of St James's would fit this image perfectly. The cemetery was cleared and became a public park in 1968.

From Gambier Terrace I walked back along Hope Street, past the art college, to Falkner Street. When they were first married in 1962, John and Cynthia moved into a flat at No. 36 Falkner Street, near the grand Blackburne Arms pub on the junction with Catherine Street. The flat was rented by Brian Epstein, who let the couple stay there as his wedding present. Did Brian live there, or was it just convenient for him? Another flat, another tiny slice of Beatles history. I stood outside and took photographs of the old houses and the cobbles, trying to omit the lines of cars. I couldn't see John being particularly happy in this flat, the forced domesticity, so close to the pubs and studios of his student life. Falkner Street hasn't changed at all since the early 1960s, or even the 1860s, apart from the fact that the small tram link was removed when Liverpool got rid of the trams in the late 1950s. It is a cobbled street, and the scars left by the tracks' removal can still be seen. The houses are nearly 200 years old, three-storeyed and terraced, with flights of steps running up to a bright front door and wrought iron balconies on the first floor. The pavements are still flagged with giant sandstone slabs, and the street lamps are still housed in cast iron Victorian lamp posts. The street seems to have retained its iron railings as well, perhaps because to

Falkner Street.

remove them would have made the street more dangerous, especially during a blackout. These streets are routinely used in films and TV programmes that need a period setting. Liverpool is the second most-filmed city in the country, the first being London.

I know these streets well – there were many clear Beatles links, even the trail itself – and yet I felt that this moondogs in bohemia landscape eluded me. It seemed a series of half-places, temporary stops during nights on the road to somewhere else. When I lived here in the 1980s the gloomy streets often reminded me of the loneliness of *Across the Universe*, with its lines about wind in letter boxes and rain in paper cups, or the overcoat isolation of *Two of Us*. Yet this time there seemed nothing permanent, nothing substantial, about their time here. There were just borrowed rooms, rented flats, a closed art college and a school that is now a performing arts college. Perhaps history does have momentum, I thought, perhaps the Beatles story was gathering speed here, approaching the escape velocity they would need to leave Liverpool, first for Hamburg later on in the summer of 1960. I didn't know, I just felt that the shadow landscape had slipped past me without my understanding, that the buildings were solid enough but that the lives had roared through them and gone.

It was getting dark. I stood on Falkner Street staring at the lights of Hope Street. The lights came on behind me, flickering and anxious, reflecting on the cobbles, which were starting to shine in another thin Liverpool rain. Hard and vulnerable girls started appearing under the pale street lights, walking on the spot as if waiting for a lift, standing on street corners. The red door of No. 36 opened quickly then closed. A hunched John Lennon scurried along the road towards the Belvedere for a quick half, leaving Cynthia at home asleep in front of the radio. I decided to wander down to the Cracke for a glass and see if anybody was singing in the War Office.

Beatle City Journeys

The old city is a whirl of dreams, of yesterday, today and tomorrow, of narrow streets, steel towers, old cobbles and mobile phones. The past is all around us, tangible, tantalizing, sometimes visible. I stood in the light rain outside the maternity hospital on Oxford Street and thought about Mimi's story of running six or seven miles out to Newcastle Road through the Blitz in October 1940 to tell the Stanleys that Julia had had a baby boy. Someone checked the records and Liverpool wasn't bombed that night, so Mimi's Blitz was a myth, but the drama of her running up Smithdown Road as the bombs fell is a better story and perhaps has a kernel of emotive truth to it. The building looked like a set from a war film, the War Office, all sandbags and parked staff cars. It is now offices in the middle of the university, with a plaque to commemorate John's birth. On a journey in or out of town I also managed a walk around the other Beatle hospital, Walton, the place where Paul was born in June 1942, although I didn't see a plaque. It is an enormous building, grand, isolated, ruinous and unapproachable. The old part is now apartments, with a newer medical building in the grounds. The rest is wasteland, derelict, overgrown streets engulfed by trees, mist and foxes.

Old Maternity Hospital, Oxford Street.

Walton Hospital, 2010.

There are more of these hidden places rooting the Beatles in the landscape of the city. Mount Pleasant has the old registry office where John and Cynthia were married in 1962. Is this the same registry office where Alf married Julia in 1938? It is now offices, this nondescript Georgian building, recently threatened with demolition for a road that didn't happen. The café in Clayton Square, where both wedding parties celebrated, has long gone, but Beatles landscapes flood the city now that Liverpool celebrates them. Walking through town on my way to Mathew Street, I passed Lewis's, where Paul had a part-time job, and Blackler's, where George trained for a few weeks to be an electrician. I remember the old tram shelter at the Victoria Monument, the old paving pattern laid to resemble tramlines. As one of Liverpool's meeting places I used to meet

The old registry office, Mount Pleasant, on a rainy day.

Victoria Monument, Derby Square.

friends here off the No. 5 bus, the bus John used to get into town. He once sat here with Thelma Pickles, an early girlfriend, for a conversation. And I remembered one cold rainy night sitting in the window of the Jacaranda, when four skinny boys in black walked past along Slater Street carrying guitar cases. Perhaps they were looking for a gig, perhaps they were actors, but in their hunger, their urgency, their razor-cheekboned rock 'n' roll determination, I saw how haunted this city is. Liverpool is dotted with these small memories, our history, these moments in time that tie us to place and event.

From the remains of Great Charlotte Street – which used to have NEMS premises – I walked down towards the other NEMS building on Whitechapel, thinking of old Liverpool street markets and St John's before the new one obliterated the old street pattern. I thought of concrete canyon back streets, devoid of character – Tarleton Street, Williamson Street, poor, unloved Leigh Street. The old NEMS building now houses the offices of Rex Makin, Brian's hard-working solicitor. I turned and turned again through this district of old back streets, slotted between narrow walls of towering dark brick with thin strips of grey sky above them, and dreamed of what used to be here, what has gone and what they would have known. Trams and green buses, Greenwoods and Hendersons, mackintoshes and trilbys, greased back hair and Brylcreem, barrows and cobblestones. The past can flicker and fade, wax and wane in the old city, becoming solid in a dark moment and then disappearing like smoke when the sun shines. Tom Slemen records these hauntings, his dark city full of ghosts, more real than the present day. And I was too familiar with the past not to let it seep into the present.

On an empty Lord Street I stopped to watch trams and old buses rumble slowly past the bomb sites, the fields of flattened rubble, high walls blackened by smoke and car parks full of Austins and Morris Minors. I had a pocket of unfamiliar old money, awkward, burning a hole. In an instant the pavements were full of people again, more mackintoshes and trilbies, pencil skirts and stocking seams, pearls and

No buses, no trams – the Pier Head, 2010.

twin-sets under light coats. Somewhere down by the docks I could hear a hooter, a steam whistle. I sat for a moment on Stanley Street, on Eleanor Rigby's real bench, thinking how strong some Beatles art can be. Eleanor is faceless, anxious, the loneliness in us all, the melancholy in their songs made visible. Tommy Steele, another 1960s crossover, made the statue of her in tribute. Buses and cars rumble past below me on long-ago Whitechapel, and an impatient horn sounds as a fruit barrow stops the traffic, slithering on a patch of cobbles. I walked slowly

Tommy Steele's Eleanor Rigby Statue, Stanley Street.

Button Street.

SUTTON
STREET
STORAGE
E.J.PRICE
& Co

onto Rainford Gardens, Button Street, following a dark, battered old van. Somewhere I still have my tin Sgt Pepper badge, four inches across (designed for a very wide lapel) bought by my mother in 1978 from Probe Records. My mother, who loved new music and danced in the Rialto in the 1950s, welcomed into the heartbeat of post-punk 1970s Liverpool.

These are very Mathew Street, these hauntings. Time is a sea of holes here, unable to hold things firmly. The borders between what was here and what is here are indistinct, allowing thoughts to slip through and the past to be imagined and then touched. I was there quite early, and the streets were waking slowly. White van deliveries and early electricians arrived, along with scaffolding boys, checked sleeves rolled back in the hope of office girls. Standing with notebook and camera, as invisible as a tourist, I could smell thick coffee on the breeze, a blast from a basement coffee bar half a century ago. The light metal chairs were being put outside to catch early visitors and tourists looking for breakfast. The waiter looked up at the thin sunlight, brushed his apron and went back inside. The pubs were closed and being cleaned ready to open at 11am. This is an old Liverpool tradition, polishing the brass and engraved glass before opening time.

I had forgotten how much I loved being in the city this early. Setting out their stalls, the fruit sellers called to each other across a half-empty pedestrianised Whitechapel, the electricians whistled at the girls and disapproving char ladies polished worn brasswork and emptied their mop buckets onto the streets. This seemed a strangely European echo, something from Amsterdam or Hamburg. The black leather ghosts of the band turning in their sleep somewhere behind the stage. Mathew Street is a street of narrow places in giant buildings, with long runs of rooms disappearing into the backs of other buildings. It is a Victorian rookery, almost a dreamscape. The sun warmed the slates but not the cobbles and the sky was slowly clearing as the offices started to wake up. Strip lights flickered and hummed, computers whirred into life. The

Mathew Street, 1925.

streets smelled of coffee from tiny bars, the chit-chat talk of *Eastenders* and *Coronation Street* echoed and the streets slopped with dirty soap suds. The sun was just up over the rooftops, over the scatterings of pigeons and the occasional seagull. The rooftops were unchanged,

Mathew Street, May, 1925.

unvisited, in 50 years, the slates glistening in the rain, the chimneys empty and unused. The roofline of Mathew Street is strangely scruffy, overgrown with weeds, as if the city's new life hasn't reached that high and the tide of tourism hasn't reached the roof yet. TV aerials lurch over the slates, the remnants of advertising peel slowly in the rains and the cool sunlight. Redundant iron canopies still protect pulleys and chains, rusted solid, swaying gently in the light wind and untouched since 1965, waiting for crates of pineapples and giant sacks of bananas. These tall, stern buildings with their narrow doors, barred windows and thick brick walls used to be fruit warehouses. I watched deals done on street corners, barrow boys hauling high barrows of fruit and the clatter of iron tyres on hammered cobbles. The streets are narrow, streets two centuries old, fruit warehouses built over market gardens that ran down to the creek. The fruit barrows on Whitechapel are part of a long tradition. Spare

Mathew Street.

brickwork is plastered with posters featuring giant lips, silhouetted naked women and famous faces advertising nightclubs, events, bar nights and glamorous parties. The sky is criss-crossed with lighting wires, turning the whole of Rainford Gardens, Button Street, Mathew Street into a tram shed or a pub garden ready for the Mathew Street Festival – 300,000 people come for three days of non-stop music from a constant, excited roar of new bands, old bands, covers bands, and tribute bands from all over the world. And even early in the morning, early in the year, Mathew Street had slow groups of early tourists. These dark Cavern cellars are the holy of holies for Beatles pilgrims, because here the music started. They were here for the music, the love of the music, the sounds that changed their lives when they first heard the Beatles, perhaps like the penniless John Lennon wandering home and hearing *Be Bop A Lula* or *All Shook Up* for the very first time, hearing his destiny calling to him from a strange window.

I wondered what visitors made of this street. There is nothing here – what was here has gone. The street's pubs are more genuine than the Cavern. There some things unobtrusively hidden in the street fabric, but not much. Yet in a bricked-up window high on the wall overlooking the Cavern is almost the only genuine piece of Beatles art in the whole city. Arthur Dooley's *Four Lads That Shook The World* is a sinister, spiky, shrouded Madonna, elongated and faceless – representing Liverpool as mother – holding long loops of – what? Rosary beads? Chains? Cobwebs? She clutches three struggling mop-headed babies, a barbed comment on the city's stranglehold on the band and how cities refuse to let go. There are only three babies because Paul has grown Wings and flown off.

On its own the sculpture would be dark, gloomy and unsettling, but it is drowned in kitsch. The bricked-up window has been painted in red and blue, with bricks highlighted to focus our attention on the sculpture. Above the Madonna's head is a false Liverpool street sign saying 'BEATLE STREET' and 'LIVERPOOL FOUR' in smaller letters, a play on Liverpool districts and the four boys. Below her is a similar sign saying 'FOUR LADS WHO SHOOK THE WORLD'. The cheap letters 'JPGR' have been screwed to the wall around the figure. Worst of all is the spray-painted doll in swaddling clothes with 'LENNON LIVES' on the halo. The text of his 1971 song, *Imagine,* is mounted below the doll, and a strange and oddly beautiful poem based on the Lamentations of Jeremiah sits uncomfortably to the Madonna's right. How much of this mess is Arthur Dooley's work? As a whole it looks like a makeshift roadside shrine, faded and neglected.

I watched the visitors take photographs of each other outside the Cavern doorway or against the original site of the doorway a few yards down the street. It is just a niche in the wall, a fire escape, a board explaining how the original entrance site was rediscovered from a photograph of a man opposite the Cavern entrance, standing in a shadowed doorway with a chipped brick, which was still there when they came to make something of the old nightclub. History in Liverpool pivots on such small details, the chip in a brick relining a street, even a whole city. This is street history in its purest form, the history of buildings creating landscapes and shows how easily they shift and change in the city, and how easily they disappear.

Further up the street is the statue of John Lennon slouched against the wall, chubby and comfortable, smug, middle-aged. He was there for the visitors to be photographed next to. It is a long way from the Jurgen Vollmer photograph of Lennon at 21 in a 1961 Hamburg doorway, cocky and aggressive, which was used for the cover of his 1975 *Rock 'n' Roll* album. Lennon thought that this picture captured 'the beauty and spirit of the Beatles,' their rock 'n' roll contempt for the everyday, the conventional, the accepted way of doing things. Normal life goes on while the band stare out into a new world from the sooty brick terraced streets of the past. Perhaps. If Arthur Dooley had been commissioned to create the 'beauty and spirit' statue, something sharper, darker and more sinister, something a lot more rock 'n' roll, might have happened on Mathew Street. But Liverpool Beatle City is a clean, safe place with nothing too deep or serious, a place that has chosen its art and its histories carefully.

Yet still everyday Mathew Street is a haunted place, her ghost stories celebrated and in plain view, divided into light and shade by a sudden opening in the clouds. The bright modern street still stands on one side, but in the cobbled shadows outside the Cavern the dark van appears again, and, unloaded, fades away. A queue of young people snakes past the fruit dealers and the barrows, the girls in high beehive hairdos – starting to be brushed downwards, cut short and flicked sideways – the boys with proto-moptop cuts and leftover sideboards. Everybody is in black and white or white and black, the surviving pictures bleached and over-exposed, turning faces into masks, dividing the city further into light and shade, as if the film could not keep up, could not keep pace with the speed of light, the speed of change. These anxious teenagers would be grandparents now. Suddenly the queue shifts, moves forward, and they are in, a clatter down a tiny flight of stairs. They are in a room of sweaty walls and far too many people, with quick-fire DJ chat from Bob Wooler. The bands are squeezed under one arch like the end of an

Mathew Street, 2010.

Mathew Street, 2010.

John Lennon Statue, Mathew Street.

'Four Lads' sculpture, Mathew Street.

alleyway, as if they couldn't escape, as if they were going to be shot. The arched roof is low, the bricks running with condensation, and the band is already playing fierce, pounding music for this raw lunchtime performance. 'In Liverpool,' said Ritchie many years later, 'the Cavern was the place to play with any band. There was a lot of screaming in there…' Jim McCartney fights his way through the crowd and throws a packet of sausages onto the stage for Paul, that night's Forthlin Road meal. Brian Epstein sits at the back with Alistair Taylor, suit and tie at odds in a world of hairspray and eyeliner, staring into his future, hearing his destiny as sure as Lennon or Robert Johnson. In the Cavern jazz fought a rearguard action with skiffle, which lost the battle with rock 'n' roll. And the whole club lost the fight with the railway; in the early 1970s Cavern was demolished for something to do with the Liverpool underground. The sun goes behind a Liverpool cloud and the image starts to disappear. The last girl turns and fades, and the wall closes behind her.

I was left on Mathew Street, melancholy for a moment, staring at the wall like a madman and thinking of the girls I would never dance with, of their journeys through time, and how old and dead this all was, how far these Beatlings had taken me from the real modern world of friends and family. But then me and the camera were bumped into by two laughing girls who looked about 15, on their way back to work, perhaps, or skiving off school, all laughing eyes and a flash of wit. Part cheeky come-on, part street humour, part old-fashioned taking the piss, this too is a Beatles landscape, invisible, ubiquitous and defiant. I realized again how rich this background is, this fast urban wit and these off-the-cuff jokes, none sharper, funnier or crueller than Liverpool's. As they said about John Lennon, you were cringing inside and helpless with laughter at the same time. The wordplay of 'Oh, it's been a hard day's night' is still everywhere in the city, defining the Liverpool panorama, humour and frowning dour-faced love of words. 'What are you laughing at?' 'Nothing.' 'Didn't think you were…' It's not what is said, it is the way it is said, the delivery, the timing and the razor response; a second later and it wouldn't have been funny. And, of course, by the time I had thought this and then something witty to say, they had gone.

I walked to the end of Mathew Street, where it joins North John Street. Fruit warehouses give way to large 'palazzo' office blocks, gigantic grimy Victorian buildings in solid Italian style. In the basement of one of these the first Beatles shop opened in the late 1970s, a place to buy original Beatles badges and swap rare albums, the first inklings of the modern Beatle City. That shop has gone, grown up, moved appropriately to Mathew Street, and its silent doors now face the giant A Hard Day's Night boutique hotel, Liverpool wordplay made real. It is a whole city office block renovated as a luxury hotel, liveried commissionaires by the front door echoing the famous mid-1960s image of a smiling John Lennon outside a public toilet, dressed as the doorman. The hotel is modern and smart, with smoked glass and Beatle art in every room. Four leaden statues of the boys wave to invisible crowds from the façade.

St George's Place, 1957.

But I wanted to turn away from the constant white-noise-scream of modern Beatle City, I wanted back streets and coffee bars and uncertainty. As the lunchtime crowd went back to work, I turned from North John Street back to an older, less visible city.

A forgotten Liverpool ripples out from these Beatle places, a landscape of buildings and youth culture. In the late 1950s and early 1960s the city seems to have been alive with jazz bars and coffee bars, all different and unique but all part of the same mood. Some of this landscape survives, invisible in plain view, whereas some has quietly slipped under. How to go back to that place, those times? How to squeeze down tiny flights of stairs into cramped vaulted rooms packed full of young people, nurses and students, factory boys, jazz fans and early rock 'n' rollers on makeshift furniture drinking coffee or soft drinks? It was easy in those days – rent a cellar, spend a few quid on paint, make some furniture, buy a tea urn and a coffee machine and you're away. Some made it, expanded and stayed the course. Others didn't, running for a few weeks before exploding under their own internal pressure. This is a Liverpool mood, this have-a-go attitude. Perhaps it is a city thing – we have the space, let's do something with it, like Mathew Street in the 1970s. Clubs and bars sprang up and lasted a few weeks or months, as they still do in this city. A floating vibrant scene and a carefree mentality, insubstantial and fleeting, those 1960s cellars were noisy, sweaty and throbbing with loud music, hairspray and teenage hopes of sex. They came and went in a whirl of can-do and music, the Cassanova Club on Dale Street and London Road, The Odd Spot, the Wyvern, the Way Down, the Iron Door, Yankel Feather's Basement Club, the Sink Club, with its numbered membership plugs, Rory Storm's Morgue Club way out in Broadgreen. Names of magic, defiance and monochrome 1960s beauty.

The money ran out, the venue licence was demanded or not renewed, a newer place opened. Basement clubs became basement store rooms again, the murals still on the walls, the lights switched off. Scenes change

The White Star.

and trends move on. Places and times overlap, buildings are reused and rediscovered, like the Pillar Club, the Sink Club, the Jacaranda, but still there is a whole invisible city of lost coffee bars and nightclubs from the 1950s, the 1960s, even the 1970s and the 1980s, dark cellars in the city, which are closed now and silent, the drip of water like condensation from an overworked tea urn. Rooms used now to store boxes and crates are haunted by a faint smell of aftershave, sweat and perfume, a crackle of early electricity. These places deserve a book of their own.

I was back on Mathew Street, which was cooling and darkening, lights coming on. Workers were starting to catch the early buses home. I had walked and thought all afternoon and it was getting late, a time for ghosts and witchcraft, and my familiar city-melancholy

The Grapes.

was returning. A sudden flurry of wind blew a flyer against my leg advertising a new venue, and I thought it said 'FRESH FROM HAMBURG'. I looked up, puzzled, as a dark figure slipped down the back street ahead of me back onto cold, dark Mathew Street and then turned into the Grapes to raised voices and roars of smoky laughter – as good a choice as any. City walks should end with a pint to break a mood, a connection with the past, and here I was spoiled for choice. I used to drink in the White Star but I thought to try an early pint in the Grapes, sit on the Beatles' bench and look at the Beatles wallpaper, this most tangible of Beatles landscapes, where they sat. The White Star and the Grapes are official on-the-trail Beatles pubs, but the Beatles drank in all the local pubs, as most bands will have done. There is a strange mythology about John Lennon drinking in Liverpool pubs, as if, like Dylan Thomas, he found pubs an escape from the everyday, as if he was banging his head on them as an alternative to distance, escape and flight. Ian Sharp had stories of his increasingly wild behaviour, the constant threat of violence, of beatings escaped by the skin of his teeth. In the Grapes there are photographs of them sitting over dark pints of Guinness or brown-and-mild, solemn, unsmiling, impossibly young. Here, too, there was a mood of increasing speed, of time slipping away. From Mathew Street and the Cavern they moved slowly out to London, America, the known world, leaving Liverpool behind. The city has chosen to be haunted by the Beatles, by their times and their absence. Turning my collar against the sudden evening wind, I walked towards the Grapes, thinking of Paul McCartney on the bus with his guitar and his sausages. I slipped through the door, imagining – remembering – cold, wet nights in golden pub rooms that smelled of wet wool and sweat and were full of smoke and laughter. As I sat with a Guinness, I thought of times overlapping, rooms at the back of back-street pubs, rooms hidden from the dark 1950s streets, remembered the unsteady last-bus cobbles slick with rain and litter, unswept fruit peelings and flyers for nightclubs.

Donations to the National Trust

On my last day in the city I woke to thoughts of light filtering slowly through old glass, opaque and stained, a pattern of blood-reds and greens and yellows moving slowly across linoleum and a threadbare carpet. I lay wondering about the same sunny, half-past-six light far away on Menlove Avenue. I heard the birds singing in the empty garden and wooden gates closing as early people left for work, and saw the early traffic, the pale ghost of a tram and a vanished hedge.

I gave in and became a pilgrim. I slipped onto the Beatles' trail of time, places and people that flows invisibly through the city. It was strange to be a tourist in my home town. I had no interest in paying to see the famous places and I could see the not-so-famous places for myself, so I joined the National Trust bus ride to the preserved houses of Mendips and Forthlin Road. This seemed to be a journey into landscape in a way that riding a psychedelic bus to see Penny Lane or Strawberry

Penny Lane tramcar waiting room, 1926.

Field would not. It was a more intimate journey, a less general view of the city. But it did mean that I never got to ride through Liverpool on the Magical Mystery Tour bus.

In Liverpool sometimes the old city is reached through the new. To see the 1930s house on Menlove Avenue and the 1940s house on Forthlin Road we met at the Jurys Inn, a new hotel on the old King's Dock site, the essence of new, popular, non-threatening Liverpool. When I was there the Wheel of Life was still erected between the Inn and the Echo Arena, one of the gigantic ship-shaped buildings on the new waterfront. Nothing here was more than 10 years old. The Albert Dock – itself an old structure given new meanings and new uses – is now framed by modern buildings and new hotels, museums and apartment blocks. In contrast, the afternoon tours run from Speke Hall, a rambling Tudor hall next to the airport. George remembered Speke Hall from his childhood. Here the process would be reversed, the 1950s would be reached from the 1550s. Time flows like water in Liverpool. In this city, past and present and future coincide, overlap and gently collide.

I climbed aboard the bus with the other pilgrims – British, American, German,

The old from the new – the Liver Buildings and the Albert Dock from Jury's Inn.

Spanish – and the driver, Andy, gave us ID badges and said, politely but firmly, 'sorry, there's only one choice of music on this bus,' and he put a Beatles compilation CD on. Listening to it all day – and having to concentrate on the driving – he no longer heard the music, but I heard the old songs, songs I have heard all my life, with fresh ears, as if for the first time, listening to it for work, for poetry. I saw the city to a soundtrack of their more famous pieces of music, the city unrolling around us as if in a film, the achingly familiar music defining the landscape as never before. Liverpool looked loved and shabby, full of mad people and happy girls, emptiness, beauty and squalor.

The journey from the city centre took us through a landscape of obscure Beatles' history, the places I had spent the last few weeks laboriously finding, exploring and documenting. We passed the site of the David Lewis Theatre, where they did an acoustic gig to 100 people in 1961, near Head Street, where John's mother was born in 1914. On Upper Parliament Street we passed the end of Hope Street/Gambier Terrace, where John lived with Stuart Sutcliffe. We drove past the site of the Rialto and the New Colony Club on mutilated Berkley Street, the prostitutes and the strippers and the afternoon drinkers long gone. As we turned onto Princes Avenue I looked along Upper Parliament Street and thought about the New Cabaret Artistes' Club, where the Silver Beatles supported Janice the Stripper in the long-ago summer of 1960. Where is she now, I wonder? We drove slowly along Princes Avenue, whose houses were built by George's grandad, past Rosebery Street and the site of the first less-than-successful Quarrymen gig in June 1957. We carried on past High Park Street, where Ritchie lived and went to school, alongside Princes Park, where he walked to secondary school and once spent a whole day drawing patterns in the snow. On Croxteth Road I glimpsed Sefton Park, where Alf met Julia, and Ritchie lost his virginity. And on to Smithdown Road and Sefton General Hospital, where Julia's body was taken to, the same hospital where Cynthia gave birth to Julian, the whole road the redundant heart of *In My Life*. Greenbank Drive

Surviving tram shed, Smithdown Road.

Synagogue followed, an early venue and the setting for Brian Epstein's funeral, and then Garmoyle Road, where Cynthia used to live. The minibus drove past Wavertree Mystery, George's Park, past Holyoake Hall, another early venue, and past the remains of John Lennon's tramsheds. Then we were at the nondescript traffic roundabout of Penny Lane and along Allerton Road – the McCartneys would have shopped here, perhaps in the Woolworths where Cynthia went into labour with Julian – and on to Menlove

The synagogue, Greenbank Drive.

Holyoake Hall, Smithdown Road, an early Beatles venue.

Avenue, where Mimi and perhaps John walked to see the Stanleys and where his mother died. It was a route soaked in history and Beatles stories, but there are probably many more echoes on this ordinary Liverpool journey. And so to Mendips.

The house is set back from the pavement, which is in turn set back from the road by a wide grass verge. The trees and shrubs are mature around the houses now, after nearly 80 years. Menlove Avenue ran straight as an arrow in each direction on this bright, sunny day, the trees waving in the slight breeze and the mid-morning traffic was light. We were dropped outside the house and met by the curator, Colin. Ours was the first tour of the day so his work day was just beginning, but he would

Cherry blossom and tower blocks – Menlove Avenue, 2010.

Mendips.

already have had an hour or two of ordinary Mendips life, seen the early morning light they saw, filled the house with toast smells, Radio Four, the noise of the washing machine and then tidied the public house to ensure it looked its best before our arrival. Both houses are seen as if the family has left for work and school and we have broken in; the breakfast dishes have been washed and put away and the tables have been scrubbed, the door banged behind the last person to leave, and the house has fallen once more into a comfortable silence. Colin told a good story and there was a palpable sense in Mendips of Mimi's presence, her strong mind, her disapproval, perhaps her social anxiety. She had, after all, come a long way from the streets around the Anglican Cathedral where she grew up. Uncle George – softer, kinder, more affectionate – was a shadowy presence, as he is in Beatles stories generally.

Mendips strongly reminded me of many houses I knew as a boy growing up in south Liverpool, especially my grandmother's house on Dartington Road. I was reminded of old fence panels, worn and bleached bone dry by 40 years of summers, thin, dusty, summer soil, the anxious trimming of hydrangeas and lawn to within an inch of their lives. But also French windows leading into the garden, raspberry canes, and a sense of peace and calm away from the city. Indoors, I remembered the strangeness of old-fashioned rubber-padded washing machines and other people's kitchens, the quiet cool magic of tiled pantries, wire mesh on windows, and all those 1950s colours, a palette of whites and greys, muted greens and creams. The colours of the Liverpool buses. By the time of my childhood these old houses were being modernized. Mimi's generation was starting to die off, and younger people were buying these small semi-detached houses, burying the older elements beneath flowery wallpaper and shag-pile carpet.

It is an unusual process, the restoration of a house 70 years old to a point when it was 20, a house important for five or 10 years because of the people who used to live here. I was curious about the minute, almost forensic peeling of the modern world away from a house, the disappointments, the unexpected survivors. Lino beneath carpet, the history of odd doors, a Belfast sink brought in from the garden, cupboards and doors from neighbours' skips. The delicate precise recreation of the past, a celebration of the intimate history of an ordinary house. This is the professional, historical, archaeological side to the work I do with old streets and vanished buildings, but while they are looking for history, I am looking for poetry. Some things from Mimi and George's time here have survived: the bookshelves in the front room, the wooden porch, the stained glass and some of the doors and fittings. I saw the small shelf running around the hall, just above the picture rail, reminding me of the willow pattern china that I have just inherited from my grandmother. Mimi had her Spode here, her Crown Derby.

The front room at Mendips had pictures of Mimi's mother, Anne Millward, as both a young and older woman. These were the only family photographs in the house, and I would have liked to have seen more. Perhaps this domestic reality is a step too far for the Trust and the visitors, most of whom, after all, are here because of John Lennon and not his grandparents. Any family pictures were in albums and not on the walls; Mimi's sister in Rock Ferry, Julia in the garden there, John with his cousins. There were none of Pop Stanley, whose face I have not yet seen; instead there were many beautiful, tasteful monochrome pictures of John as a young man, during the Mendips years, John with Julian in the garden or with Cynthia, and then of the Quarrymen, and the Beatles in Hamburg. It was easy to forget the history of these rooms, the big and little dramas, and the people who lived here – the lodgers who stayed the whole time John lived here. Cynthia, who lived briefly in the front room downstairs with baby Julian. Perhaps even kind Uncle George. John argued with Mimi in these rooms; George brought him supper upstairs after he had been sent to bed. The stairs creaked as John climbed them late at night, trying not to wake Mimi. He cut the grass outside for his pocket money and was photographed on it in his *Just William* school uniform, crumpled and unbuttoned, many times. There is no room in restored houses for the past to be imagined, and I could not see John Lennon at five years of age, slowly climbing the stairs with his panda under one arm and his teddy under the other. Or perhaps I did see him, slipping through legs, amused but puzzled, climbing into a bed in a world – the past – invisible to me. I stood on his landing and tried to see him.

One of the oddest stories I found about Mendips was the story of the plaque. In the early Beatlemania years John had Mimi's famous phrase 'The guitar's all right, John, but you'll never make a living at it' (or 'The guitar's all right as a hobby, John, but you'll never make a living at it,' depending on the text) engraved on a small plaque and screwed secretly to the front wall of Mendips. Some 14 years later, living in New York, he told her about it in a telephone conversation. The family went out into the garden, cut back the shrub under the window and found the plaque. Mimi took it with her when she left Mendips in 1965 and gave it to her nurse when she was terminally ill in 1991. The nurse, Lynne Varcoe, subsequently sold it at Sotheby's to fund her nursing studies. And so the plaque disappeared. It is a story so peculiar I could barely understand it or believe it – the dates don't add up, the time is awry, and it is a story so oddly hidden it had to go in the book.

John's room was surprisingly small, a box room over the hall. It has the controversial pictures of Elvis and Bardot, the copies of *Alice in Wonderland*, the tip of the iceberg of his childhood library, and the speaker system that allowed him to listen to the radio in his room. Perhaps it was here that in 1956 he first heard *Heartbreak Hotel* on Radio Luxembourg, a life-changing moment, although I prefer the image of the scruffy poet drinker wandering home through Toxteth and suddenly hearing rock 'n' roll for the first time.

I stared out of the window onto a quiet Menlove Avenue, a road so impressed on my memory it is like a thumbprint, and thought about the darkest of John Lennon's stories, the death of his mother. I have known of this story all my life, it seems to me, perhaps from walking along

Menlove Avenue with my mother in the late 1960s to see her friend, Peggy Martin, further along towards Woolton. Standing briefly in his window I could see Julia chatting with John's friend, Nigel Whalley, at the gate. She turns to go, still laughing, and checks for cars. The road is empty. She walks to the middle of the dual carriageway and through the hedge around the old tramlines. Distracted this time, she doesn't check the traffic and steps out in front of a car, which hits her full on. Nigel turns to look at the awful noise and sees her body fly through the air, a moment of horrified, slow-motion confusion. He shouts for Mimi and runs across the road. Mimi's reserve breaks and she howls and cries and screams, waiting for the ambulance. They take Julia to Sefton General Hospital, but she has already died. I was afraid of this story, afraid of its horror and its consequences for the young John, then only 17. The driver was also young, an off-duty police officer called Eric Clague. He was acquitted of any crime but was suspended, and he later resigned from the force. He became a postman in the early 1960s, and – a horrible irony – his walk included Forthlin Road, where he delivered sacks of Beatles fan mail. There is another possible link with the McCartneys as well. The Beatles in Ireland website has some of the McCartney family tree, and Paul's great-grandmother was born Jane Clague. It is an unusual name, Clague, an old Manx name. If this is right, then there is the distant possibility that the man who killed John Lennon's mother was related to Paul McCartney.

I turned back from the window, from 1958, and realised that we were being given 10 minutes to wander around on our own to open cupboards, touch the light switches. I looked again at the old family pictures and the back garden, thinking of the small boy that lived here, finding his story sad and unsettling. I looked for the seven-year-old John in the garden on a cool sunny day in the late 1940s, but the house was too immaculate to imagine John and Mimi and George here. The past was immediate, unreachable, literally unimaginable. It was time to go.

Colin, friendly but distant (Mimi would have approved), had told us about the acoustics in the porch that John and Paul both liked. It was one of the few places Mimi would let them play, although what the neighbours must have thought, and it has a bright, bathroomy sound with an element of glassy echo that suggested a recording studio. 'People sing in it occasionally,' he said, suggesting a very Mimi pleasure and disapproval at the same time. I paused in the porch on the way out and caught the eye of the woman behind me. 'Are you going to sing?' she asked. 'Oh, go on.' So I sang the opening lines of *Eight Days A Week*, faltering, then strengthening, too quiet, too awkward. But I did it and I am glad I did it. I had stood in too few real tangible Beatles places on these journeys, although I crossed their roads many times, but for that short time I sang in their footprints.

The bus took us to Forthlin Road. I half expected it to take the Fletcher's Farm road over the golf course, John's old way to school or to see Paul, but instead we went the rainy-day route down Yew Tree Road alongside Calderstones Park. The day was turning grey, the sun was fading, and Forthlin Road was as quiet as on my last visit, walking the area to see what they saw. I had forgotten the curve of shops on Heath Road, their nearest tobacconist, perhaps the grocer and the fishmonger, and the small Catholic church of St Bernadette, Mary's local church, where her funeral took place in October 1956.

Paul and Michael's mother, Mary, lived in this definitive McCartney house for only a year until she died of breast cancer. Both houses and both stories are haunted by the early deaths of the boys' mothers. 'I would have liked to see the boys grow up,' Mary McCartney said before going into hospital for the last time. Paul and Michael were about 14 and 12 at the time and felt their mother's death keenly, but the extended family rallied around and helped out with housework and shopping and cleaning, and gradually the dreadful absence in their lives was calmed and soothed, if not healed. So it is Jim McCartney who is the adult presence in this house, with the piano and his musical encouragement, with his dahlias and snapdragons. It was Jim who washed their smalls in

No. 20 Forthlin Road.

the old sink, caught startled in Michael McCartney's famous photograph. Here, too, there are no ordinary family pictures, but lots of Michael's stark iconic images, their family and young days captured and imprinted onto the house, film images of real people on the walls.

The house is smaller than Mendips, a chalk mark or two down in the social landscape the Beatles helped to destroy or at least realign. Visitors comment that it is warmer, it feels more homely, and perhaps coincidentally the curator, John – who bizarrely resembles Paul McCartney – has none of Colin's friendly reserve, he is warm and chatty. Paul and Michael asked for some tangible presence of their parents in the house, so a plaque was erected over the front door remembering Jim and Mary, reminding us that this was a home even though it is now a museum. It is the just-down-the-road presence of Michael and Paul that gives this house its life. Mendips is beautiful, but everyone connected with that house seems to be dead.

There were more archaeology stories here, stories of the original drainpipes and doors, the sink that came from the garden, the old cupboards that were found in a Forthlin Road skip, the kitchen floor tiles that are original. And, appropriately enough, there is more awareness of photographic image. The drainpipe in the back garden that George, Paul and John stood next to uncertainly, awkwardly, to be photographed in off-duty jeans and leather jackets is there, and the deck chair placed in the garden replicates the image Michael snapped of Paul unhappily strumming the guitar, through the dining room window. Visitors are not allowed to sit on it, not since a fat guest sat down and crushed it, to some anger and hilarity.

The garden and the outside WC overlooks the Police Training College, which used to own huge areas of land here. The house itself is built on the old police fields. 'We used to sit on the concrete shed in the back yard and watch the Police Show every year for free,' Paul remembered. 'One year, Jackie Collins came to open it and we were entranced at the sight of her comely young figure.' There are many more direct memories in Forthlin

Road, the past is more present, perhaps making the house seem warmer.

There was not enough time to spend in either house. There was just enough time enough to read the information, see the rooms and ask questions, but not enough to simply be there, to absorb the atmosphere, the mood, the sounds and sunlight. John Lennon spent hours writing and drawing at the tables in Mendips; he knew the light on the walls, the way it moved as he worked. He would have heard the neighbours' dogs, the old trams rattling past outside, the birds in the garden. Paul McCartney knew the way the light filled the Forthlin Road kitchen and the hour it reached the garden until 11am. He would have heard the milk float outside, the neighbour cutting the grass. It is not practical to give people more time, as with four tours a day the next one is always snapping at your heels but I would have like to have longer to sit and to see what they saw. The way sound and light move through a house forms some of our deepest and most subconscious memories, and they do not need restoration.

Forthlin Road may not have piles of books or laundry, but it has a piano. Jim bought a piano from Brian Epstein's father on Walton Road, which Paul still has and still uses. The one in the front room at Forthlin Road is a similar one but not the original. John the curator said, 'we do have a piano, can anyone play?' And a shy Spanish girl said that yes, well, she was taking lessons. 'Oh you can play for us later,' said John. And on the way out of the house, in the 10 minutes we were given for private time and photographs, I found myself in the front room with John, a couple of the tour party and the Spanish girl. 'Here's the piano,' said John, and he played the bang-bang-bang repeated note from *A Day in the Life*. 'Go on, have a go.' The piano was unused, unloved and out of tune, a piece of set dressing, but the Spanish girl sat and coaxed the *Moonlight Sonata* from it, awkwardly at first, then with more confidence, riding easily over the out-of-tune notes, flooding the rooms with Beethoven. She finished nervously and for a moment there was a stunned silence, filled only with birdsong and a murmur of voices outside. Then we applauded and congratulated her. Someone made the obvious *Roll Over Beethoven* joke, and perhaps other people remembered John Lennon's comment that *Because* was basically the *Moonlight Sonata* played backwards, as a good piece of embroidery can be seen from either side of the cloth. Hearing it played in that house was beautiful, unexpected and moving; a rare, precious moment.

The bus collected us from Forthlin Road as the next party of visitors arrived. I was silent on the ride back to King's Dock, finding this history heavy, the sudden, ancient, almost intrusive sense of loss for Julia and Mary, how long-gone all these people suddenly were – George, Mimi and Julia, John, Mary and Jim. I wanted to be ridiculed by the chatty, bouncy girls from Mathew Street, have a pint, listen to a band that didn't sound like they were from the 1960s, or all three. I found the journey back through these Beatles landscapes moving, tracing as it did their journey from dockland immigrants in reverse – their last homes, impeccably restored; through areas they knew well; past parks and streets of early

The old city from the new – King's Dock, 2010.

stories; past demolished venues and old homes; to the docks, to Saltney Street, standing for all Beatle family incomers from Scotland or Ireland, for all immigrants, and so for all Liverpool families. I thought of the private homes of Admiral Grove and Upton Green, their 1960s history built over, wiped out. I thought of poor, unloved Madryn Street, sounds moving in rooms hidden behind thick steel shutters. But Mendips and No. 20 Forthlin Road, preserved as they are in aspic and melancholy, mark a point of departure, a leaving of the city. This was where John and Paul lived until they left the city forever and their fame closed it behind them, preventing their casual, ordinary return. On the bus back into town I thought of the day when the boys left these houses for the last time, closing the door behind them one ordinary afternoon, or perhaps sneaking out under cover of darkness to avoid the fans. Yoko's introduction to the Mendips guide says that John spoke about the past constantly, this landscape of old places and old friends, the world of *In My Life*. She felt that she knew Stuart Sutcliffe and knew Mendips, John had spoken of both of them so often. Paul came back with his brother to see the restored house, a man stepping back into his own history. He was perhaps given the sense that, somewhere behind him, the past, his pre-Beatles past, was recoverable, immediate. Perhaps that is why Michael and Paul wanted the plaque commemorating their parents putting up in the hall, over the front door.

The tours are over by 5 o'clock, the houses quiet again. The grass starts to recover in the gardens, to unbend. The afternoon light strikes a different wall and starts the slow slide through the rooms towards evening. The curators can tidy up, make sure the houses are clean and start to think about their evening meal. All day these houses are full of voices, stories and laughter, but only after the visitors have gone do they start to really come to life, with the low murmur of the radio or the TV, the ching-chong of a laptop switched on to check emails or headlines, coming to life with a burst of music. And the cooking smells coming from the tiny kitchens, the click of a kettle switching itself off, the sausages grilling in the cooker.

Afterward – The Footsore Notes

This is a book of journeys and stories, not a book of conventional history. Nevertheless, some of it has been researched and stories have been chased up and verified wherever possible. Newspaper links were mainly found on-line and provided background, but Ritchie's memory of a cold Admiral Grove comes from a *Daily Telegraph* article by Andrew Perry from April 2010, where he talks about a new song *The Other Side of Liverpool.* Here are some books I found useful:

My ancient, crumbling copy of Miles's *The Beatles In Their Own Words*, still stained with iron ore from Lake District holidays thirty years ago; Ray O'Brien's excellent book *There are Places I'll Remember*; The Beatles' monumental *Anthology*; Michael Braun's sharp, immediate *Love Me Do*; Pauline Sutcliffe's book, *The Beatles' Shadow – Stuart Sutcliffe and his Lonely Hearts Club*; Ringo Starr's book, *Postcards from the Boys*, which is full of small stories and family journeys from when he had become Ringo; Albert Goldman's *The Lives of John Lennon*, which is perhaps not always reliable but which is firmly rooted in real places and times; *The McCartneys in the Town Where They Were Born* by Kevin Roach, which took early McCartney stories and family seriously, and *I, Me, Mine* by George Harrison. I found a beautiful edition of this in the publishers' clearance shop in the new St John's Precinct. I also re-read Hunter Davies' 1968 book, *The Beatles*, and my battered 1977 edition of the Beatles' lyrics, which I first read nearly 35 years ago as lonely, disjointed poetry. David Bedford's book *Liddypool Birthplace of The Beatles* looks superb but came out too late for me to steal any ideas. Perhaps arrogantly, I didn't read any of the modern giants of Beatles literature, other than on-line, but one afternoon in the Records Office I did see the magical name 'Lewisohn' in the list of people who had borrowed a file of obscure photographs. I felt I was on the right track and in good company.

Most of the everyday information came from the internet, especially useful when looking into a subject as popular as the Beatles. A quick Google search for 'The Beatles' produced over 35 million related sites. Some of these will be duplicates, links to pages on the same site. Individually, John and Paul tie with nearly 13 million links each, with George at six million and Ringo at nearly three million. Many parts of the one story could be found on different sites and in different places, the same story told as it were from different points of view, like Michael Byron's genealogy work, which brought him into contact with the Lennon family. Small descriptions flicker across the net; on one site I found an account of Mimi crying in the kitchen when John came home from his Scottish relatives in 1955, having to tell him that Uncle George had died. Then it was gone and I couldn't find it again, as if that picture, that memory, can no longer be traced. All four Beatles have websites of news and new releases, and they have captured their domain names so that their name is followed by .com (www.paulmccartney.com/ and so on). Pete Best didn't feature in these pages as strongly as I would have liked, but he too has a website at www.petebest.com.

Wikipedia seemed to have limitless information well-supported by research and earlier articles. All the principal characters in the story have entries in this encyclopedia. Here are some of the other general websites that I found interesting:

http://inacityliving.piczo.com/?g=1&cr=7
This is a fantastic archive of what seems like thousands of old Liverpool images. I lost several afternoons in there.

http://www.beatlesource.com/savage/main.html
The Savage Young Beatles website is dedicated to images of the band, day by day, before 1963, as well as stories about recordings, bootlegs, venues etc.

http://www.lennon.net
This is the official site of the Liverpool Lennon family and attempts to give a sense of broader family history to John's life.

http://www.iol.ie/~beatlesireland/
This was a starting point for the band's Irish connections and it has some fascinating stories about all four Beatles and their family links with Ireland.

http://brakn.com/jack1.html
This is Michael Byron's Lennon page, part of his family history.

http://www.beatlesireland.utvinternet.com/Irish%20Heritage/paulheritage.html
This has good stories about the McCartney and Lennon families in the north end of the city and was the starting points for my Saltney Street and Breck Road/Heyworth Street meanderings.

http://www.cavernbeatles.com/blog/dezo.htm
This has more information on Dezo Hoffmann on Allerton Golf Course. Rick Alan has done sterling detective work on these images and laid to rest a niggle in my mind – I always knew that the leaping images weren't taken in Sefton Park but didn't follow it up.

http://www.silverkgallery.com.au/The%20Beatles/thebeatles.htm
This site has Dezo Hoffmann's astonishing original movie film of that day on the golf course and also quiet, eerie footage of George Harrison driving through a south Liverpool full of Ford Populars and Mk I Cortinas.

http://kenwoodlennon.blogspot.com/2009/03/kenwood-kenny-everett-acid-errrgolf.html
Kenwoodlennon is a fascinating site, but this link is to Kenny Everett's beautiful, truthful and hilarious LSD story, taken from his

autobiography *The Custard Stops at Hatfield.* This site is linked to http://lifeofthebeatles.blogspot.com which took me to Barry Miles's book *Paul McCartney: Many years from now* in which I found the Jackie Collins story.

http://www.britishbeatlesfanclub.co.uk/features/2007/0821_book_imaginethis.html
John's sister, Julia Baird, has a different slant on Mimi and the other Stanley family, and a startling and angry interview with David Bedford can be read at this link. The fan club site is full of interesting and unusual stories. Julia's father John 'Bobby' Dykins was written out of Stanley family history, but John might have known his parents as well.

http://triumphpc.com/mersey-beat/beatles/johnlennon-menloveavenue.shtml
The Stanley family story at the beginning of 'The Empress and the Admiral' chapter comes from John's cousin, Stanley Parkes, in this interview with Bill Harry. A strange footnote to this story is the road sign for Head Street, which is still bolted to an isolated stretch of railings buried deep in Otterspool Park. Bill Harry's thoughts on the *Sunday People* article of July 1960 is taken from his website, **http://www.merseybeat.com.**

Head Street sign, Otterspool Park.

http://www.spencerleigh.demon.co.uk/index.htm
Spencer Leigh is a Beatles/Merseybeat expert – more afternoons can be lost here.

http://www.icce.rug.nl/~soundscapes/VOLUME12/Interview_McGrath.shtml#Noteref18
The Liverpool black clubs and musicians of the late 1950s and 1960s, and their contribution to the Beatles' sound and background, deserve a whole book, but this article by James McGrath is a fascinating start.

http://www.britishbeatlesfanclub.co.uk/features/2008/0328_lynn_varcoe.html
I found the Mendips silver plaque story bizarre and inexplicable. Here is the quote from Wikipedia, under 'Mimi Smith'. 'In later years, Lennon would jokingly remind Mimi of her comment, and after The Beatles' success he had a silver plaque engraved with her words, which he secretly installed behind a bush underneath a window of the cottage. He called her one night from New York asking her to check behind the bush for a surprise. The bush had to be cut down as it was overgrown and there, stuck to wall was the plaque saying "Music's all right, John, but you'll never make a living out of it". This was some 14 years after he had it installed. When later asked about the plaque, Mimi would say that Lennon had it made for her husband George, and not her' (**http://en.wikipedia.org/wiki/Mimi_Smith#cite_note-LynneVarcoeInterview-35**). The dates don't add up for this story – Uncle George died in 1955 and Mendips was sold in 1965, yet John rang Mimi from New York, where he moved to in 1971. But the plaque did exist. Lynne Varcoe, Mimi's last nurse, was given it by Mimi in 1991 or 1992 and sold it at Sotheby's to raise money for her nurse training. Perhaps that's why Mimi gave it to her. The link above tells her side of the story.

http://www.thetimecapsule.org.uk/TimeCapsule/098231E9AF3B4160 8C7E503A38AD6CC1_D55D7B9D222E4780A856A8F10B4CBAD9.htm
This huge, unwieldy link takes you to the memories of people in Woolton in the late 1940s, a glimpse of John's childhood and another world.